POETIC THEFT

C.M. Masner

Copyright © 2017 by C.M. Masner

This is a book of poetry, fiction, and nonfiction. Any resemblance to specific events, or characters, living or dead, unless properly named, is coincidental.

All rights reserved. Published in the United States by C.M. Masner.

No reproduction or use of this original content can be made without express written permission by the author.

"Multicolored Circle" by Wassily Kandinsky
appears on the cover with permission from
Yale University Art Gallery
All rights reserved.

Edited by   Leeanne Seaver
Book Design   REACTOR

ISBN 978-0-692-87400-4

for the better angels in others who helped create the better angel in me

~ **C.M. Masner**

Contents

	Poetic Theft	9
	Art Work	10

I.	**Beginnings**	**15**
	A Plea for Ecology	17
	A Ride in the Country	18
	A Voice of Memory	19
	Attempted Suicide	20
	Being a Star	21
	Cabin Sleep	22
	Confusion	23
	Inside and Outside	24
	June 4, 2016	25
	Lost in the Canyon	26
	Minor Leaguer	28
	Paradox	29
	Poemsong Prayer Meeting	30
	Remember the Moon	31
	Sentiments	32
	Slavesong Free	33
	Snow Walk	34
	Souled	35
	Southern Banquet	36
	Sunday Service	37
	The Sentimental Truth	38
	To A.R.	39
	Words Worth Saving	40
	Words Worth Saving II	41
	Writer for Hire	42
	Yesterday's Tears	44

II.	**Love**	**47**

Grace	48
A Bad Poem That Got Me Laid	54
A Certain Kind of Love	55
A Fine Little Piece	56
A Light Romance	57
A Prayer for Love	58
Anna's Love Note	59
Beloved	60
Dance by Me	61
Dark Angel	62
Goodbye	63
Handmade Moments	64
Holy Roller	65
Hopeless Romantic Wants Hook-Up	66
I Saw Her Face Today	67
Intimacies	69
It Was Just a Kiss	70
Kiss of the Bridesmaid	72
Lovelife	73
LoveMaking	74
Lovers' Rain	75
Missing You	76
Moon Lovers	77
Pretty Pleasures	78
Reapin' and Sowin'	80
streamtounconsciousness	81
Summer Dresses	82
Sweet Talk Girl	83
The Good Nights	84
The Seduction	85
This is Just to Say – Goodbye	86
Till Death Do Us Part	87
To Rob, from Sabe	88
Tracy	90
Winter Lover	91

III.	**Love and Difference**	**93**
	The Button Man	94
	Charlie	99
	Kemosabe	100
	The Revelation of the Rose	101
IV.	**Difference and Love and Race**	**103**
	The Snot-Nosed Kid	104
	Across the Years	111
	Children of the Sun	112
	Dreamdust	114
	The Whole Truth	115
V.	**Difference and Love and War**	**117**
	My Conversation with Max	118
	Collateral Damage	131
	Joe's War	132
	The Morally Just War	134
VI.	**Death**	**137**
	Fertile Ground	138
	A Grandson's Story	141
	A Lifetime	142
	A Matter of Time	143
	A Matter of Words	144
	A Thing of Beauty	146
	Death at Any Age	147
	Death Words	148
	Empty Spaces	149
	Freedom	150

Gravesong	151
Heaven Is a Communist Country	152
Last Kiss	153
Last Words	154
Lifewalk	155
Life and Death	156
Little Gifts	157
Metaphors for Infinity	158
My Epitaph	159
Nights	160
The Losers' Art	161
The Whippoorwills Were Singing	162
There Was a Day	163
Whispers in Time	164

Poetic Theft

because I took a line from time
a line from time took me

Art Work

A human life is a work of art. This is the ideal. An individual human life is an individual representation of all finite human life. It therefore becomes complete and is always incomplete. It is an internal creation of the individual as mediated by the external societies of which the individual is a part. All lives, like all artistic creations, are bounded. A life begins and ends. In between these ultimate boundaries, there is a middle life of more beginnings and endings that is nonetheless continuous until life ends. It is the role of an educator to help the individual learn, from the beginning of life through the end of life. The representation of this learning is the artistic creation of an individual, and the societies of which the individual is a part, as manifested by the individual and those societies.

The ability of an individual to realize life as a work of art depends upon the health of the individual and the societies of which the individual is a part. These are interdependent. The healthier the individual, and the societies of which the individual is a part, the greater will be the ability of the individual, and the individual's educators, to realize the artistic creation of the individual's life. It is therefore a duty, of individuals, educators, and the societies of which they are a part, to secure the greatest health possible for all individuals and societies.

Democracy does not guarantee a healthy society in the short term, but it is indispensable for the maintenance of a healthy society in the long term. A society, no matter how well fed, clothed, or housed be its individual members, cannot be healthy if its individual members are not otherwise justly treated as free individuals. Democracy does not condemn revolution. Democracy does not worship revolution. Democracy manages revolution in order that individuals and societies may seek optimum health. The alternatives are anarchy and tyranny, both of which are reciprocally inevitable in a society that is not sufficiently just and free. The artistic fulfillment represented by an individual life grows best in societal soil that is neither too loose nor too solid. This is democratic soil. To thrive, individuals and societies must be allowed to change, but individuals are rooted in the traditions of the society into which they are born. The better the knowledge of individuals of those traditions, and how the power of those traditions is manifested, the greater will be an individual's capacity for productive and positive growth. It is therefore a role of the educator in any society to support and seek a democracy that fosters a justice and a freedom that is created out of this kind of learning, and to be a primary leader of individuals in the process of this kind of learning.

Democracy does not guarantee equal quality. Some human lives are shorter than others—no matter what the quality of the democracy. Human lives experience different degrees of disability and suffering—no matter what the quality of the democracy. The paradox of the perceived existence of a God worthy of that name is that it presumes that death, disability, and suffering could be ended while still maintaining the capacity for human individuality and growth. Until the occurrence of such an event, it is the role of the educator to enable individual and societal human life, no matter what its challenges, so long as there is life. The educator must fight any evil in art, and any suffering in art, while still ennobling a life that is tragic.

In order to best help the individual learn, the educator must bring the world to the individual, and the individual to the world. The means for doing so will vary with the age and abilities of the individual learner. The younger and less able will need more help from the educator in bringing the individual into contact with the world. Initially, it matters less the subject matter which the individual seeks out to begin this journey of learning, than that the individual be helped to understand that all subject matter is connected to all other subject matter, in the tradition of knowledge of the societies of which the individual is a part. The world is whole. Human beings only divide the world into parts because that is the only way they can begin to try and understand the whole of that world. Thus, the most fundamental of all learning is philosophy, and the most important of philosophical learning is moral philosophy. The educator must help the individual develop an understanding of the why of existence, and of the proper relation of the individual's existence to the larger existence of which the individual is a part.

The educator must intelligently observe the individual in interaction with the world, so as to help the individual reflect on the individual's own observations of the world, and the individual's subsequent interactions with that world. This observation by the educator requires the diligent attention of the educator, and the commitment of the educator to achieving the best dialogue possible with the individual learner. The best dialogue possible means the most honest dialogue possible, which means that the educator is open to the new learning which reflective dialogue produces. The world is not a static place. Change is eternal. The educator must also be a learner in the individual's journey of discovery, if that journey is to produce the best learning possible for the benefit of the individual, and the societies of which the individual, as learner, and the individual as educator and learner, are a part.

The educator must provide the individual with interpretations of the educator's observations of the individual's interactions with the world. Thus, the educator, while also being a learner, must be more learned than the individual being educated. The dialogue between learner and educator cannot be appropriately rich or complex, and thus the educator cannot appropriately lead the individual learner out into the world, unless the educator's observations are more informed by prior learning than the individual learner who is being educated. Being so informed is a fundamental, although not a sufficient, condition that enables the educator to fulfill the educator's role of leading out the individual into the world of which the individual is a part.

It is not enough for the educator to observe and interpret the individual learner's behavior in the learner's ever expanding world. The educator must evaluate that behavior, and share such evaluation with the individual learner. This evaluation by the educator must include the educator's moral judgment about the worth of that behavior. Individual learners can best become appropriate moral beings in the societies of which they are a part, if they are given possession of the moral judgments of those educators that are entrusted to lead them out into the world. All learning must be moral learning, and a primary role of the educator must be to communicate the moral judgments of the educator, in order to help the individual learner in the learner's acquisition of a moral philosophy, with which to engage the world, and grow in the world.

In order that the individual learner best accept the moral judgments of the educator, it is a necessity that the educator be a person of moral integrity. There being no perfect human beings, moral integrity does not require perfection. It does require a willingness both to question principles and to hold fast to principles. The world is filled with ambiguity, but ambiguity can be no excuse for a failure to be morally courageous. Moral integrity requires that an individual nonetheless be willing to make decisions in a world of uncertainty. The educator must help the individual learner to intelligently develop the moral integrity and courage necessary to make decisions in a world where decisions can always be questioned.

Moral integrity also requires that the educator fight the corruption of the ideal of truth, wherever that corruption is encountered. The educator must enlist the individual learner in this fight. Whether there be one truth, or many, the educator must enlist the individual learner in being ever vigilant against accepting proposed truth based solely on the assertion of power by those in possession of power. The truth survives the temporary possessors of power. Truth cannot be named for an individual learner; the individual learner must give truth a name in order for the individual learner to truly possess that truth. A society that asks more of an individual is not a democratic society, or a free society, or a just society, sufficiently worthy of being named democratic, or free, or just. Such a society must be resisted, and it is the role of the educator in such a society to lead the individual learner in that resistance.

There is no escaping ambiguity, and the requirement of living in an ambiguous world. An individual must accept that which must be accepted. An individual must change that which must be changed. An individual must learn to know the difference. This is the moral character and learning that the moral educator must help the learner make a part of the learner's individual constitution. This is the way to help the individual create a work of art that is the individual's life of which the individual can say at the end of that life I did some good in this world. It is the way of creating a good society.

Note: Sentences two, three, and four of the final paragraph are a revised statement of a formulation the original credit for which is sometimes given to Reinhold Niebuhr. However, I know of no recording, written or otherwise, conclusively documenting such a formulation by Mr. Niebuhr. ~ CMM

Section I

BEGINNINGS

A Plea for Ecology

This love-letter folded in two is looking for a flower's address.

> ~ Jules Renard, **The Butterfly**
> translated from the French by Richard Howard

I try to imagine
a world without
butterflies.
I try to imagine
a world without
flowers.
I try – but not too hard.
Where would all the butterfly poems fly?
And who would write them and why?
Mr. Renard deserves better.
And so do you.
And so do I.

A Ride in the Country

The motor hummed.
No – The motor roared.
The air smelled sweet.
No – The air smelled alfalfa sweet.
The windows were down.
In the Malibu.
Without those window dividers.
Four down make two.
The radio played something.
Something Sixties.
It was three a.m.
No – It was four a.m.
Tired, sleepy, but awake.
Beer and whiskey buzz.
Marlboro drag.
Pushing along about seventy.
Leaving my youth behind.

A Voice of Memory

"her voice was soft and sure"

from *The Pinnacle,*
by W.S. Merwin

I cannot get my mind round the end of time, but I have faith that long after W.S. and the rest of us have breathed our last, the boys will still be doin' beers and shots down at Jack's - and flirting with the local flowers, like they could bring the second coming of the morning dew. The Old Crow chasers washed down by the Pabst Blue Ribbon brews. The boys down at Jack's said they'd never heard of you, W.S. - so I read them the poem you wrote about Miss Giles, the retired teacher, going on a walk with you, when you were a boy, before you had started school. You wrote, "we could tell from our different heights that this kind of thing happened so rarely that it might not come round again." And you wrote, "she was beautiful in her camel hair coat that seemed like the autumn leaves." And you wrote, "her voice was soft and sure." The boys liked the poem you wrote about Miss Giles, W.S. The voice of the poet, the voice of his memory, like the voice he remembered, was soft and was sure. It made the flowers bloom.

Attempted Suicide

He put
an imaginary
gun
to his head
and pulled the trigger.
He did this
in the morning
and at night
and at any time
during the day
he found himself
alone
and in front of
a mirror.
In time,
he got strong enough
not to pull the trigger.
In time,
he was glad
the gun was imaginary.
The imaginary had been,
and had been not,
the enemy of the real.

Being a Star

Stars know not modesty,
nor majesty, nor mystery.
Stars know not Being.
Stars know no beings.
We are the beings of stars.
What stars can Be,
only we can know.

Cabin Sleep

The window is open.
The reading light is off.
The poetry is in your heart.

Tiny claws scratch across floor wood.
Night wings flap in the attic above you.
There is the sound of the rush of snowmelt water
against the rock of river.

The feathers of dead birds warm you.

Light reflected from the fire of life
fixes shadows in the room.
In the spaces between shadows
the light frost colors the pure cold of night air.

The dream you are going to have is just beginning.
You sleep – deep, precious, sweet, complete, sleep.

The poetry is in your heart.

Confusion

Confusion walks her carpet,
and I hear the eternal rain
at my door –
as if to say "I smiled at you,
and called you back for more."

Inside and Outside

Silence inside.
A motor hums outside.
Warming up.

I struggle to write.
I struggle to say.
I struggle to be.

It's cold outside -
Above the snow.
It's warm inside -
Below the snow.
But the world waits.
I must go.

June 4, 2016

I was born
on June 4, 1949.
I graduated
high school
in 1967 –
the summer of love.
The class of 1967
graduated 49 years ago.
We are all
the age of 67.
We re-unite in July.
The summer of love
has returned.
This encore
was not planned for
in 1967.

Lost in the Canyon

There must be some word for stars.
Some word other than diamonds.
Some metaphor for the unknown
light year destinations and
the unknown light year journeys
we will never take.

In the canyon on my back I let my
human eyes rest from north to south
and east to west across the vast
blackness of the universe where
from my most humble of views sparkled
light that had travelled through so
much time not to reach me -
but just to travel
because travel is what light does.

So many eyes over so many human years
having looked toward those same lights
in that same universe
with so much thought
and so much wonder.

I heard the river.
I tasted whiskey.
The night's breath
was bitter and sweet.

My blanket was warm.
My belly was full.
I closed my eyes
and I went to sleep.

Death will someday come to me
and it will bring to me more revelation
or I shall return to the unknowing night.
Until then I will grieve for
those I love who die before me.
Until then, God or no God –
there is the worship of wonder.

Minor Leaguer

He was good at the little wits.
But the big truths –
Well – they escaped him.
Or rather, they did not escape him.
Every major needs its minor.
It was not a popular test.
Not in baseball –
where there are
leagues of majors
and leagues of minors.
Home runs are popular –
but popular never
hit a home run.
There is a fair territory fence.
Home runners escape fences.
Critics cheer, and jeer –
and drink more beer.

Paradox

When a heart breaks
it makes no sound,
even though a world has ended.
When we take our lover
our lover takes us,
even though we were free to stay apart.
When we are born
we do not ask for life,
even though we must accept the gift of death.
We live for what we do not know,
even though we try to understand.
Paradox is the master of the heart.

Poemsong Prayer Meeting

Let's hear it for
the singer songwriters -
the musicians
the singers
the poets of song.
Let's hear it for all of us.
Sing and play.
Play and sing.
Clap, whistle, shout, and cheer.
We're alive.
Let's bend God's ear.

Remember the Moon

It has rained ice on the snow.
Your boots crush into powder.
There is no other sound
save for your breath
and the wind.
You need to get home.
Night will come soon.
You are alone
waiting for the moon.
It will not find you here long.
You will accept its fullness
from inside your cabin window -
in front of your wood stoved fire.
It will shine on the snow.
It will show where you walked.
It will do this for you
but it will not remember.
You must remember the moon
because the moon will not remember you.

Sentiments

Sentiments.
Blurs on thought.
Killer instincts.
Revenge.
Valentines forever.
Where are those
words that don't
need saying?
Where are those
words you just feel
deep inside?
The poet knows
they are not words.
That is why
she writes.

Slavesong Free

The binary is the canary in the coal mine of slavery.

Snow Walk

She walked out of her front door. She was wearing a white cotton tank top, and long legged, pink polka dotted, cotton pajamas; and pink flip flops. She could have been no more than sixteen. It was snowing big wet flakes. He saw her walk down the wooden deck steps of her home. When she got to the bottom of the steps, she turned to her right and walked into an open meadow. He could see the wet snowflakes on her hair, and on her clothes. She crossed the meadow, and went up and over a slight hill, and into some sparse woods. He could no longer see her. He was thinking it might be necessary to knock on his neighbors' door, or call the police, if she did not return soon. He did not know his neighbors, or their circumstances. He was relieved, when she appeared again, and walked back across the meadow, and up the wooden deck steps of her home. Her hair, her face, her neck, the bare skin of her upper chest and back, her clothes, and the bare skin and fine hair of her arms, were wet and flaked with white. The flush of her face surpassed the pink of her snowy wet flip flops. She walked back into her home.

Souled

If you make a deal
with the Devil
don't expect the details
to be in your favor.

Southern Banquet

Sweet tea.
The day is humid hot.
The tea is iced cold.
The glass sweats.
Cold fried chicken.
Cold sliced cucumbers.
Sweet red tomatoes,
homegrown,
sliced and cool.
Chilled deviled eggs.
A heap of homemade
mustard potato salad,
chilled.
Sliced and sugar
sweetened strawberries,
refrigerated overnight.
Lemon icebox pie.
Sweet tea and a smoke.
I can still feel the draw.

Sunday Service

The teenagers hold hands
and think of last night.
In their finest clothes today
they long to hold more than hands.
Their little brothers and sisters
slide on and off of parental laps.
The little sisters raise their skirts
without intention.

The old folks sit mostly silent.
A nod to a neighbor. A hand on a Bible.
Mildred fortes the organ.
The preacher enters.
The congregation rises.
Voices sing.

The Sentimental Truth

The truth is never too sentimental.

To A.R.

A.R. Ammons:
C.M. Masner.
Archie Randolph Ammons:
Charles Michael Masner.
I may never
equal you in rhyme,
but we will always
be in rhythm.

from C.M.

Words Worth Saving

A tear on a window pane.
Elephant birds.
I could write this line forever -
What is it that makes you cry, when you know that tears are all you have left?
His wife has been seen waiting for tomorrow at the Raven in Williston.
Braces and bubblegum don't mix.
We all cry out our beginnings and our endings.
A child of patience is no child at all.
Sad songs played on the radio
of eternal mysteries
in the twilight of our love.
The nights were cool and black.
Poetry was our only accusation.
Dreams denied were all we had left.

Words Worth Saving II

Life learns Being through being.
He preached American:
you can't have my soul – go get your own.
Poetry is a rear view mirror.
She slept like the water of the sea.
Poetry is the mystery of the obvious.
The sky is the sea and the sea is the sky.
The poet tells lies with truth.
The poet tells truth with lies.
He had been enough places
for death to take his burdens from him.
If I lived forever would beauty matter?
If I lived forever would poetry matter?

Writer for Hire

I am a writer for hire.
I will throw words
like stones
into your pond.
The words will become
many sentences
and make a bridge.

I will cross over to you.

We can then
get to know each other
a little better.
Maybe make a story
together -
or a poem that rhymes -
or not.

I expect to have
many stones left over
once I cross over.

Once I cross over
I can bring you truck loads.
There will be enough
for you
and I (I know it is me)
to make
many beautiful paragraphs
together -
I think that would be wonderful.

I am a writer for hire.

Please hire me.

You will get what you pay for.

Yesterday's Tears

Memories
like yesterday's tears
flow from me
once again
to become
words
upon a page.

Section II

LOVE

Grace

I.

My wife told me she was gay. Well, bi-sexual, actually. After ten years of marriage and two kids, she had figured this out. Figured it out with the help of a Master's degree in Feminist Studies from the University of Kansas. She said she could no longer live the heterosexual married life with me. She was divorcing me, and moving in with what would be her new partner, Jackie. She might have other men as sexual partners in the future, but I could not be one of them. There was too much "emotional baggage" between us. She was taking the kids. We could be "friends."

I confess, I did not see this coming. In retrospect, you'd have to say that my soon to be ex-wife, Shelley, was really good at lying in bed. Meaning, she was really good at convincing me she was a good lay. Or, rather, really good at convincing me that she was enjoying being laid, by me. All of those "Oh my Gods" and "Yes, baby, yeses" were, in hindsight, merely bad bedroom dialogue in what I thought was a good marriage. This is the conclusion that I reached. My confidence in myself was no longer that confident.

In the face of this domestic disaster, I did what any good man would do. I hit the road. I filled a suitcase with a change of shirts and pants, and lots of socks and underwear, threw it in my classic cherry black and white 1963 V8 Ford Falcon, pointed it west on I-70 out of Lawrence, and left. I would be back in a couple of weeks, I told Shelley. She might be leaving me, but I would never leave the kids. I just needed to get away by myself for a while. I sold insurance on commission, and my boss, Tom, a sensitive and understanding heterosexual guy like me said, "Take as long as you need."

II.

I was driving drunk. I had a case of pop-a-top canned Coors in an ice chest beside me, which I was chasing with swigs out of a bottle of Wild Turkey, and I was pushing my little Falcon down the interstate at about 80 miles an hour, chain-smoking Marlboros, and listening to country music on the radio. I was behaving very badly, and I wasn't being very creative about the way I was doing it. A part of me was hoping to crash, and that part of me got its wish.

I was just west of Hays, and it was past sundown. The weather had been good when I left Lawrence, but it was awful now. It was January, and there was a mother of an ice storm in the making, something I would have known if I would have been in any shape to be paying the attention I should have been paying to the weather information that was being broadcast periodically over the radio. Anyway, frozen rain started hitting my little Falcon, and the pavement beneath it. I did have sense enough to slow down to something below fifty, which still wasn't slow enough, given that I was drunk. What I needed to do was stop driving, which I did, with the help of a skid, a ditch, and a telephone pole.

III.

I woke up in what I was able to recognize as a hospital room. I was sore all over, and realized that my mouth was swollen up and swollen shut. I hoped I still had teeth in there, but I didn't know for sure. The painkiller they must have given me must have deadened everything. I could move my arms and legs enough to know that they must not be broken. I could see, and hear, and smell, so that was good news. The room had that antiseptic hospital smell, and the storm was still going strong outside. The hard, frozen rain was testing the hospital room windows, and lightning flashes licked up the darkness in the room through partially opened Venetian blinds. Flashes followed pretty quickly by cracks of thunder. I was in a room by myself, as near as I could tell.

She must have come in my room sometime after midnight. I saw the swing door to my room swing open, and I saw a young woman dressed in white enter the room. As the door swung open, light from the hallway silhouetted her figure. She was a well curved young woman.

She was wearing a knee length white dress with shoulder length dark hair. She walked to the end of my bed and flashed a small flashlight on my chart. Then she walked to the side of my bed nearest the door and saw that I was awake. "We don't normally get patients this young," she said. I was thirty-five. "Let me get some lotion and a towel and I'll give you a back rub." I nodded my head yes. Then I turned over on my stomach.

She untied the loosely tied laces on the back of my hospital gown. I turned my head towards her and watched through the lightning flashes as she squeezed some almond scented lotion into her hands and then watched her rub her hands together gently. Then she began rubbing my back. Her fingers were long, soft, and slender, with finely tapered nails. She went up and down my back lightly with her lotion laced fingers. The soreness in my back softened. I don't know how long this went on, but I knew she would have to stop eventually, so I decided to see if I could extend the pleasure. I turned over and pulled my hospital gown down in front.

She took her hands away momentarily and squeezed some more lotion into her palms, rubbed both her hands together, and then began massaging my chest. This went on for a while, and then it occurred to maybe I could just move her hands a little farther south. I thought I could tell by the way she was touching me that she would probably be agreeable, but I decided to hold back. I don't know why I decided to hold back, but I've always been a little shy about making the first move with women, so maybe that was it. Maybe I was just afraid I might be wrong and that she would reject my move, or accuse me of doing something improper. She was being nice to me. Maybe I didn't want to risk offending her. Anyway, I didn't do it. Like I said before, my self-confidence was not the best.

After a while she quit. She rubbed the lotion off her hands with a towel, put her right hand on my forehead, and said, "Go back to sleep now." Then she left the room and I went back to sleep.

IV.

When I woke up, the sun was shining steady into the room. Someone had turned the slats fully open on the Venetian blinds. I could now see a clock on the far wall which read 9 am. Shortly after I woke up, a middle aged man in a long sleeved white shirt with a stethoscope around his neck came through the hospital room's swinging door. He picked up the clipboard chart at the end of my bed and then came around to the side of my bed.

"Good morning," he said. "I'm Doctor Martin. I know you can't talk, and I know you're sore, other than that can you shake your head and tell me whether you feel okay?"

I nodded my head.

"Good. The ambulance brought you in here about 8 pm last night, after your accident. We kept you on pain medication and took x-rays. We found nothing broken, and you didn't lose any teeth. Your mouth will be sore and swollen for a couple of weeks. I'll give you a prescription for the pain to take with you. Otherwise, you can check out as soon as you get dressed. You were lucky. Oh, and we called the number we found for your wife on your checkbook. We told her what happened and that you were alright, and that you would be able to check out today. There's a sheriff's officer waiting for you by the check out desk, which is down the hall to your right when you leave this room. He can tell you about your car. Okay?"

I nodded my head. The doctor smiled at me and left. I got up, got dressed, and left the room.

V.

When I got close to the check out desk, the sheriff's officer saw me and came up to me and introduced himself as Deputy Johnston.

"The tow truck hauled your car to their garage in Hays, about ten miles back east up the road. It wasn't totaled, but you won't be able to drive it till it's fixed. I can take you to a car rental place in Hays, after you come down to the sheriff's office with me and complete some paperwork about the accident. We ticketed you for DUI. You'll be needing to make arrangements to come back for a court appearance, unless you settle it before then. Do you understand?"

I nodded.

After listening to the deputy, I walked up to the check out counter to check out of the hospital. I didn't say anything, but I handed my insurance card to the woman behind the counter, and she took it and made a copy of it. Then she gave me some papers to sign, and I signed them. Then I motioned with the pen I was holding in my right hand that I wanted to write her something.

"You need some paper?" she asked.

I nodded my head yes, and she brought me a note pad.

I wrote, "Who was the nurse who took care of me last night?"

She looked concerned. "Why? Was there some problem?" she asked.

"No", I wrote. "I just want to thank her."

The hospital receptionist smiled.

"That would be Sister Grace, sir. But I'm afraid she's at confession right now. You can leave her a message and I'll give it to her. Otherwise, you'll have to come back in about an hour, or this evening when she comes back on duty."

"Did you say 'Sister Grace'?" I wrote.

"Yes, sir," the receptionist said.

"Sister Grace meaning she's a nun?" I wrote.

"Yes, sir." The receptionist smiled at me. "Would you like to leave her a note?"

"No," I wrote. "Please just tell her that I said thank you."

"I'll do that, sir." The receptionist smiled at me again, and I turned from the counter and went out the front door of the hospital with the sheriff's deputy. As I turned to get in the passenger side of the deputy's cruiser, I saw the sign above the entranceway to the hospital. It read, "Sisters of Charity Hospital."

VI.

I went with the deputy to the sheriff's office and completed the necessary paperwork. I got a court date for the first Monday in March, but I also got the telephone number for the county attorney. I expected to try and plead out with a fine. I had no prior convictions other than parking tickets.

The deputy took me into Hays. The work on my Falcon was going to take about a week and cost me a couple of thousand bucks. I rented a Mustang and headed back to Lawrence, sober. I was feeling pretty good. My self-confidence was back. Eddie Baker still had it. Eddie Baker had caused Sister Grace to have impure thoughts.

A bad poem that got me laid

Soft, warm, wet, wild, and waiting wonder.
Slowly sinking, savoring more than slumber.
Tasting, touching, telling tales of tenderness.
Close, clinging, cleaving, and kind caress.
The night knows no other need so necessary.
And only in parting find we a passion weary.
So let long those lacing limbs linger and last.
Far away from the place where passion has past.
Silently, sweetly, seek the shelter of my skin.
So that you might make me richer than other men
who cannot claim your quiet, quavering kiss.
But can only imagine a mystery they must always miss.
Then let me slowly stray safely to your side.
That we in sleep our love may confide.

A Certain Kind of Love

She must have had ten years on him – or more.
He never asked.
But she asked if he wanted to know.
He said no – he didn't care.
She was uncertain.
She had been uncertain
when he slipped off her dress.
Unlike her wedding ring,
which never slipped off.
He whispered for her a fantasy.
A fantasy of a one stoplight town
and a '57 Chevrolet back seat,
and of a Catholic girl in a pleated skirt,
and a Baptist boy in a pressed white shirt,
and of a first time.
She liked that.
She went from uncertain to certain.
Afterwards, they lay and smoked Marlboros.
Then, the morning came,
and she was uncertain again.

A Fine Little Piece

Why write anyway?
Tomorrow it will all be gone.
Hell – it's all gone now.
Or rather, it has never been here.
Whatever it is.
I keep thinking of her dimples
and her teeth of white
and her smile
and her freckles.
I haven't yet been able to
look deep straight into those eyes
in a good light.
I'm thinking they are brown
but they could be blue
or maybe even green.
What poetry we could make together.
Writing be damned.
If I could get wet deep hard inside her
with those legs around me
licking those breasts.
What a sweet little fuck
she would be.

A Light Romance

Sunlight, moonlight, starlight – and don't forget the scented candlelight.

A Prayer for Love

"It was like being inside a prayer."
That's what he said about fucking her.
Only – he didn't say fucking.
Charlie was lost in romance.
Charlie was lost "in love."
Charlie always got real romantic –
just before he broke his heart.
I didn't have the heart to tell him –
but she had prayed for me, too.

Anna's Love Note

It is probably not wise
to write poems to dead women.
The living are trouble enough.
But only cowards and wise men
try to avoid trouble.
So here I am
A poor poet and a bad philosopher
professing to you my love.
And please know
I am not one of those men
Who tries to find himself
in the greatness and beauty of others.
But it is not my fault
that you are beautiful and great.
It is only my fault that I found you.
For that I will take the blame.
Although, of course,
In the way of such things
It was another fair one
who passed me the love note
You wrote –
"Let him not desire my eyes,
Prophetic and fixed.
He will get a whole lifetime of poems,
The prayer of my arrogant lips."
Kiss me Anna.
Please, please kiss me.
I am all puckered up.

Love note from Anna Akhmatova
Passed to me by Judith Hemschemeyer

Beloved

Captured like a drop of rain
tasted by her touch.
Released by the body of her heaven
just for the nourishing of me.
For nothing more nor less
than everything that mattered,
all that was worth my being
was when she spoke my name.

Dance by Me

The young women walk by
in their shorts and their short dresses.
Young legs and painted toes
dancing by me.
Always dancing by me.
I grow old while they dance by me.
Please, young dancers, dance by me.
Please, dance by me.

Dark Angel

Dark haired and dark eyed.
She was an Angel who believed in angels.
We had nothing in common.
Except that I wanted to devour her.
…Like the Devil.

Goodbye

You know
and I know
what we
know.
What could be
so simple
and so difficult.

Handmade Moments

I held
your hand
like you
were a sparrow
that had fallen
but now
was safe.
That was what you said.
That was real pretty –
I said.
That was poetry –
I said.
I wish I could
write you poetry –
I said.
Poems were just moments –
you said.
Moments made by hands.

Holy Roller

My religion is sex.
The body of a woman
is my church.
I never keep the Sabbath holy.
But I do worship every day.
I am no Baptist.
You don't have to drown me.
I will still be saved.
I am no organized sinner.
Every time I enter the church,
I get that old time religion,
all over her again,
and again,
and again.

Hopeless Romantic Wants Hook-Up

To be with her
where words became lovers
and lovers became words.
To be with her
where desire became knowing
and knowing became desire.
To be with her
where all calls were answered
and no text replied.

I Saw Her Face Today

I saw her face today.

I had not seen that face
in forty years.
It was not the same face.
It was the same face.
The face that appeared
before me
forty years ago.
The face on the body
that knelt before me
as I sat before her.
The face on the body
that held my hands
with her hands
on my knees.
The face that held
the lips
that I kissed.
The face that held
the lips
that kissed
me back.

The face that held
the lips
that encircled
the mouth
that spoke
the words –
"Sometimes, I wish
I could be
two people."
She couldn't.
I saw
her face
today.

Intimacies

In the night, after making love, they shared a cigarette. The window was open and there was a breeze. He laid his hand on her warm belly. He kissed her breasts. She turned towards him and passed him the cigarette. He took it and put it between his lips. He inhaled and exhaled. "Are you okay?" he asked her. "Yes", she said. He knew this was not true. They were in their fourth year, and he knew there would not be a fifth year. He knew that she knew this, too. Still, they pretended. The sex was still good, but now it was also sad. Someone would find someone else. Then, it would be over. They had no courage to do it any other way. When they were together, the first time, he asked her if it was okay. He told her they didn't have to. She pulled him down on top of her for an answer. The second time, it was in her bed, not his. By her invitation, not his. He undressed her. The dress, the stockings, the slip, the bra, the panties. She took off her earrings. She cupped his hand, and placed the earrings in the hollow of his hand. She guided his hand to the small tray on the small table by her bed, where the earrings would lay for the night. When he was in bed with her, he turned her body gently towards him. He stroked her. He asked her if that was the way she wanted to be touched. She said yes. He stroked her until she came with a small cry and clung her body next to his. Then, he rolled her slightly, and she was beneath him, and he moved inside her. After they made love, he lay on top of her until she touched him to move, and then he moved to lay by her side. He lay by her side again tonight. He would miss her. He knew he would miss her.

It Was Just a Kiss

I was twenty years old. Rita was thirty. Jimmy was forty. Rita and Jimmy were married. Rita liked to dance. Jimmy didn't. None of that was my fault. I wasn't much of a dancer either, but I liked getting close to Rita. Jimmy was the loading dock day shift supervisor for Mickey's Trucking, which mostly did short haul jobs, in state, out of Wichita. Rita worked there too, as a secretary. She used to come to work in short dresses and pantyhose. Rita had great legs. I used to watch her every chance I got through the big window off the loading dock. Jimmy took a liking to me. That wasn't my fault either. This was just a summer job for me. I was going back to school in the fall. Jimmy and Rita liked to go for drinks after work on Fridays. They would take me along. Jimmy would buy drinks for me, even though I was underage. Jimmy would tell me to go dance with Rita. Jimmy drank. Rita and I danced. Other guys would come by and ask Rita for a dance, but Rita would only dance with me. I would dance the fast ones with her, and then the slow ones. I always figured I didn't deserve the slow ones, unless I danced the fast ones first. It was late July, and we were in this basement bar. It had been one hundred degrees hot that afternoon, and hadn't yet cooled down much outside. But in the Corner Cellar Bar, Jimmy, and Rita, and me, sat cool. Jimmy and I were drinking cold beers. Rita was sipping her usual glass of white wine. I could see the red lipstick she was leaving on the glass. Rita and I got up to dance a slow one. The dance floor was full. I found Rita and me a spot lost in the crowd. I guess that sounds like I planned it. But, I didn't. The music was loud, and we were slow dancing, and I just leaned down and kissed her. Then I slid my hands into the back pockets of the jean shorts she had changed into after work, and I pulled her closer. She was warm and soft. I was warm. I wasn't soft. When the dance was over, I touched her face. It was moist to my touch. She said, "Now you got me all excited." We went back and sat down in the booth with Jimmy. Jimmy looked at her next to him, leaned over and kissed her, and said, "You got all sweaty."

Rita called me the next day. She wanted to get together. She wanted me to tell her it was okay. I couldn't say anything for certain. She called me again the next week. She had decided against it. Rita, and Jimmy, and me went out on the Fridays that were left in that summer, but things were never the same. Jimmy still bought me drinks, and Rita still danced with me, but there were no more kisses. Rita even danced with some other guys. I don't know. I got the feeling maybe she told him. I don't know. I didn't see Rita and Jimmy again after that summer.   It was just a kiss.

Kiss of the Bridesmaid

The dresses were bridesmaid blue. The young men in the wedding party were tuxedoed in black. They wore their suits well, their backs straight, and the suit coats hanging from top to bottom without the girth of middle age to obstruct the journey of the cloth. It was a day of sun and shine, but of moderate heat. No one would sweat but the bride and the groom. The Methodist church was filled with the family and the friends of the couple, there to wish them well on their life's journey together. It was all serene. The bride came down the aisle, the Reverend recited, vows were given, and the deed was done. When kissed, the bride blushed. Pictures were taken, and then the bride left the groom to change out of her white wedding dress, and into the pretty underwear and the pretty sundress she had bought for the wedding party, and for the couple's honeymoon journey together. They had been together many times. She knew what to expect, and she was in a flush with the expectation of being with him again.

Meanwhile, the groom was also making his way out of the church's sanctuary, also to change for the wedding party and for the honeymoon road trip. The road trip would not be too long. The groom was not wanting to wait too long. On his way out of the sanctuary he stopped to kiss the bridesmaids - which included the sisters of the bride, wives of the bride's brothers, and the bride's best friend. He got to the best friend and to the maid of honor, Evelyn. Evelyn had claimed to Christina, his now wife, that he was interested in her in a way unbecoming for the soon-to-be husband of her best friend, his bride, although Evelyn could recite no advances that he had made. Christina, his bride, had believed his denial, and indeed he had made no advances, but the fantasy was real. Evelyn leaned up to kiss him. Her lips parted, and he felt the flick of her tongue, as she cradled his neck with one hand, while she laid her other hand on his chest. Then, she whispered "Congratulations" into his ear, and he again felt the flick of her tongue. And then she turned on her high heels and she walked away. The honeymoon was less than one would have hoped for, and the marriage did not last.

Lovelife

There were days when
nothing happened
because everything happened.
A hand was held.
Lips were kissed.
Sighs were exchanged.
Eyes met in knowing.
A life between beings.
The flesh
and bone
and blood
of the choices
we did not make.
The life we had –
and will never have again.

LoveMaking

He wrote love letters.
He drank whiskey from a glass.
The letters were silly.
The whiskey was warm and sweet.
What did it matter?
Perhaps he should quit.
He would never
win her back.
Words on a page.
The taste of the night.
Thinking of being inside her
while trying to write.

Lovers' Rain

It rained in the night
and into the morning.
Steady on the tin roof.
I was glad for the rain.
You were glad for the rain.
But the rain just rained.
No God was trying
to please me
like I was trying
to please you.
I could never survive
that much attention.

Missing You

Fallen leaves.
The wind blowing fallen leaves.
The breeze cool.
Voices of children.
Traffic on the highway in the distance.

The time after sun, and before dark.
Twilight time reminds me of you.
Autumn time reminds me of you.
Spending time reminds me of you.
Missing you.

Moon Lovers

I can see the full moon out my window. I hear the street noise of traffic. I would like to close the window, but the day has been hot and the night air is cool. I hear the man and the woman in the apartment below argue. She tells him to stop, she needs to sleep, she has to get up early tomorrow. I hear no words from him, and she only says stop once. I hear the sounds that lovers make in the dark. I'm lonely, but I'm glad my window is open. I know the moon that lights my room is the moon that lights the room of the lovers below me. I listen till all I can hear again is traffic. I would like to smoke a cigarette, but I have quit smoking. I can smell cigarette smoke coming from the lovers' apartment below. I wait till the smell of the smoke is gone. I lay awake in the night, thinking of the lovers, thinking of the lovers holding each other until they sleep.

Pretty Pleasures

I don't dislike pretty women.
I have stared at quite a few.
Still – pretty ain't the whole game.
Not the half of it.

You don't really know what
you are in for till
you are in the all together
without the world there, too.
Not till you have felt
skin on skin
breath on breath.

Not till she has whispered
your name in your ear
And said yes
And said please
And she has taken
All you can give
And given all you can take.

Not that pretty can't
do this, too.
Like I said –
I have stared at quite a few.
But there is really
nothing like
The sound
And the touch
And the smell
And the taste of
the night
with a woman
who knows pretty much
all there is to know about
pleasing you.

Reapin' and Sowin'

It was one of those mom and pop joints with
greasy burgers and fries
and eggs and hash browns
and specials twice a day.
Redneck farm boys were smokin' Winston's.
They talked about rain and no rain
and the ass on Marlene
and custom cutters
and cold beer
and how it might be nice to be like them cutters
and get a little pussy somewheres else
instead of bangin' Carol or Cathy or Becky
or some other local daddy's girl -
and startin' in Texas and goin' to Canada.
It was June in Kansas and the day had been warm
and they couldn't wait for the shower
and to get started on whiskey and cold beer
and so they took their burgers and fries to go.
And Marlene's boy Johnny just kept lookin' at 'em
and wantin' to be like 'em - all ten years of him
with his mom on a Saturday night
his daddy a custom cutter himself
who had already passed through.

streamtounconsciousness

softthighscurledaroundcocoabutterskin
gentleflicksoftongueswarmbreathstangledhairwetfleshhardfleshsoftflesh
dressdownoverbreastoverhipsonfloor
foreheadkissesneck
kissesfacekisseslipkissestonguekissesbraoffbreastskissed
pantsopenedpantiesoffhandsstrokingwetnesserectmoisthardinside
fingerstouchstrokeneedwantlove
thrustingtouchesmoremoremore

Summer Dresses

Summer dresses
that sun shafts through.
Shifts and slips
of pretty pastel hue.
Soft and light
and leggy up windblown.
Summer dresses are flags unfurled,
waiting to be raised and flown.

Sweet Talk Girl

A deer quivers in the morning mist
before the arrow inside her
steals her heart forever.
She told him his lovemaking was like that.
He was a goner.
Her quiver never let him go.

The Good Nights

Nights when cool air
came through the bedroom window.
Nights with the smell of wood burning
from a neighbor's stove.
Nights that were silent
because the children
had gone safe to sleep.
Nights when the touch
of her skin
was all he needed
to make him believe
that love was real.
He liked to remember
the good nights.

The Seduction

He watched her powder her breasts.
He moved from the bed towards her.

"Go back to bed," she said.
"Not yet," he said.

His hands moved round her.
His hands kissed powder.

"Go back to bed," she said.
"Not yet," he said.

His hands moved lower.

"Go back to bed," she said.
"Not yet," he said.

He neck kissed her.
He soft touched her.
He soft stroked her.

"Go back to bed," she said.
"Not yet," he said.

She turned from her mirror.

She soft touched him.
She soft stroked him.
She soft spoke to him.

"Go back to bed," she said.
And they did.

This Is Just to Say - **Goodbye**
(With apology to William Carlos Williams)

So. Willie.
You ate the plums that were in the icebox
and which I was saving for breakfast.
I swear.
You poet boys are all alike.
You use your sweet words to open us sweet girls up,
and then you use more sweet words to say you're sorry
when you want us to forgive you
for something not so sweet that you have done.
Well, I'm sorry too, Willie, but it's not just about the words.
I know the plums were delicious.
That's why I was saving them for breakfast.
Sweet words are nice, but some more plums would have been nicer.

Well, no matter. I'm leaving you, Willie.
I've found another man.
He's not silver tongued liked you,
but his tongue is sweet, and firm, and wet, and warm -
and when kissed by his lips my plums are never cold,
but they are always sweet, and firm, and delicious,
as his tongue speaks to me without words.
He is now the poet of my body, and my body is his poetry.

Goodbye, Willie.

Please forgive me.

For you, a muse, no more.

Till Death Do Us Part

The ember fire
red rich does glow
inside this night
graved deep by snow.

I think of you
and all our past
this winter's night
to be our last.

To touch of you
to touch of me
forever wish
that cannot be.

For love's last night
turned into sleep
for break of day
no more we weep.

To Rob, from Sabe

The earliest known writings of Robert Frost were four notes written during the autumn of 1886, to his schoolmate Sabra Peabody. He was twelve years old. *(Selected Letters of Robert Frost)* What follows is one of those notes, followed by a response that Sabra might have written.

DEAR SABE; I will ansyer your letter to let you know that I am well and hope you are the same. About me liking Lida better than you you are all wrong because I like you twice as much as I do her and always have thought more of you than any other girl I know of. I thought you were going to the entertainment the other night but I didnt see you there. I saw Eva Hattie and your mother there. There is no fun in getting mad every so [often so] lets see if we cant keep friends Im sure I am willing. I know I have not treated you as I ought sometimes and sometimes I don't know wheather you are mad or not and we have gotten mad and then we would get friends again ever since Westons party when I first came here. There are not many girls I like but when I like them I fall dead In love with them and there are not many I like just because I can have some fun with them like I can Lida but I like you because I cant help myself and when I get mad at you I feel mad at myself to.

FROM YOUR LOVEING ROB.

DEAR ROB; I was glad to get your letter, but I am still confused. You confuse me so much. You know I would not have said anything about Lida, if it were not for you paying so much attention to her. I am glad to hear you like me twice as much as her, but sometimes you do not show it. I did not know how you felt, so I did not come to the school entertainment the other night. I like you Robert, because you are good at football, and you are good in how you talk to me. William Walker likes me, and he is good at football, too, but he doesn't know how to talk to me like you do. A girl likes a boy who is good at things like football, and can also talk to her. Boys are so lucky that way, if they only knew it. I cannot play football. You say there is no fun in getting mad, but you know that is not why I get mad. I get mad at you when you do not talk to me in a nice way, like I know you know how. If you do not know when I am mad, I am sorry. Sometimes, I do not know myself, and it is hard for me to tell you. You say there are not many girls you like, but girls you do like you fall dead in love with, and then you say you have fun with Lida, but you like me because you can't help yourself, and that when you get mad at me, you get mad at yourself, too. I am confused, Robert. Why are you mad at me? I do not think I have done anything to make you mad at me. You say you have fun with Lida. Can you have fun with me? I do not want you to be mad, Robert. I want you to play football, and have fun, and talk to me, and be the boy I love. I want that forever and forever, but it makes me afraid to tell you sometimes, because I don't want you to make fun of me, or end up liking Lida better than me, and then we would not be friends anymore. That's how I truly feel, Rob, and I hope you feel the same way, too. FROM YOUR LOVEING SABE.

Tracy

We went for a ride in the country. In my old '63 Ford. She had her legs curled up under her in a little white and grey striped jumpsuit. She was four years older than me, but she looked like jail bait. I reached over and stroked her leg and told her how pretty she looked. How she looked like a present that needed to be opened. She smiled. "You always know the right thing to say," she said. I guess that was right. At night, that night, like all nights, she wanted me to undress her. Take everything off her. Save the panties for last. Stick my fingers in her. She'd be wet. Then I'd open her over, and over, and over again. I always felt like it was my birthday, or Christmas. Tracy was like that. She liked to give, and I liked to take. Maybe heaven, or hell, will be like that. They'll be giving and taking all the time.

I just hope that wherever I go, Tracy will be there.

Winter Lover

When I die, let me be in bed in winter,
while dreams of spring, and summer, and autumn, in my heart abide.
When I die, let me be in bed in winter,
with Spring, or Summer, or Autumn, sleeping sweetly by my side.

Section III

LOVE AND DIFFERENCE

The Button Man

He was twenty-six years old and his given name was William Francis Miller. He went by Billy. Billy was retarded. That was the word that was used in 1966.

I.

When Billy was sixteen, and a student at Frankton, Kansas High School, the Frankton High football team, the "Frankton High Fighting Tigers," took state in Division III, the smallest athletic Division in the state. It was the only time in Frankton High athletic history that a team in any sport had won a state championship. That's still true today. Billy played right tackle on that team.

The locals talked about that game then, and the old-timers talk about it now. The championship game was against Roosevelt High, the "Fighting Rebels" of Roosevelt High, an out-of-conference team that Frankton had never played. The Rebels were known for their strong defense. Their defensive line averaged two hundred pounds, and they were quick. Neither team had much of a passing game. Frankton also had a pretty good defense, so it was thought that the game would come down to who could best run the ball against the other team's defense. That proved to be the case.

The score was tied seven to seven with less than a minute to go. Frankton had the ball on Roosevelt's thirty-yard line. It was fourth down and three. Neither Frankton nor Roosevelt had field goal kickers they wanted to count on outside of a placement on the twenty-yard line. At that time, there was no overtime. The game could end in a tie. Frankton went for it. The Frankton fullback ran through the hole Billy opened up for him, beat the linebackers and the secondary, and scored. The kicker added the extra point, and time ran out on the following kick-off to Roosevelt. Frankton won the state championship, fourteen to seven.

The Frankton fullback got the glory of course, but the Frankton fans, and the fullback and the rest of the team, knew that Billy helped make the glory possible. The coaches had to adhesive tape a big "L" on Billy's left thigh pad, and a big "R" on his right thigh pad, so Billy would know which way to block when the quarterback let him know in the huddle in which direction to block. Billy did his job, blocked right on the play called, the fullback scored, and the rest was Frankton football history. Billy never learned to read or write real well, and he didn't graduate from Frankton High, except with the special diploma they gave him, but Billy successfully played his part in the Frankton Tigers championship football season.

II.

After leaving high school, Billy stayed in Frankton. There was no place else for him to go. He continued to live with his parents. He did farm work and odd jobs, like mowing lawns, and washing windows, and delivering circulars door to door throughout town, when one or the other of the local clothing stores had a sale.

Billy had a hobby that got him a nickname from the town's children. Billy collected bottle caps. He had jars and jars of them in his room at home, with the overflow jarred and put in a storage shed out back. He carefully sorted the Coke caps, from the Kastens caps, from the Suncrest caps, from the Orange Crush caps, from the Pioneer caps, and he sorted all other soda and beer bottle caps that he found and that people gave him. The members of his church, the Sacred Souls Catholic Church of Frankton, brought bags of their used bottle caps into the church's supply room to give to Billy.

Billy always wore blue denim bib overalls and carried bunches of bottle caps with him in the pockets. He made buttons for children out of the bottle caps. This was still in the day when you could find cork lined bottle caps, before plastic became less expensive than cork, and bottlers switched to plastic. It was a simple thing that Billy did. He carefully used his pocket knife to remove the cork lining of the cap. Then he put the bottle cap against a child's shirt, placed as the child wanted it, and pressed the cork against the inside of the child's shirt and against the now open space inside the bottle cap. It made a decorative button. No permanent damage was done to the shirt. When you took the cork and bottle cap off the shirt, the indentation all washed out. Little children liked it. At some point, one of them called him the "Button Man," and the nickname stuck.

III.

The limits that fate had placed on Billy were shared by another of Frankton's residents, Carrie Anne Johnston. Carrie Anne was sixteen.

Though slow like Billy, Carrie Anne was as pretty as Billy was not. Carrie Anne's hair was the color of wheat gold and her skin was soft and fair and free of blemish. Her lips were full and her teeth were white. Most of the time she was smiling. Billy was big, and pimply, with a crooked nose and crooked teeth. He mostly smiled, too, but his smile did not attract the girls like Carrie Anne's smile attracted the boys. The one way in which Billy might be said to have been greater blessed with beauty than Carrie Anne was in his eyes. Carrie Anne's eyes were not unattractive, they were a warm almond brown, but Billy's eyes were the turquoise sea blue of coral reef waters that neither Billy nor Carrie Anne would ever see. Within a face that, unlike Carrie Anne's, was otherwise unappealing, the blue of Billy's eyes was made magnificent.

Carrie Anne and Billy attended the same church, and they were friends. Whatever else Billy and Carrie Anne were made for, they were made to be friends with anyone who would return their smiles. It was therefore not surprising that they were friends. Of course, the smiles of others were not always as sincere as their own. Carrie Anne was more like a child than Billy. She was sixteen, but she acted like she was no more than a child of four. Billy made buttons out of bottle caps for her, and she smiled.

IV.

The Johnston's family doctor, Doc Taylor, had tried to persuade Carrie Anne's parents to let him give Carrie Anne a hysterectomy. He had done so because he did not believe it would be wise for Carrie Anne to experience a pregnancy or motherhood. He thought giving birth might be dangerous for her. He also wanted to free her from menstruation. Carrie Anne's parents would have none of it. While they had no intention of letting Carrie Anne become pregnant, their religious beliefs would not allow them to have their daughter made unable to have children. They would help Carrie Anne as needed with her menstruation, and they would keep her from becoming pregnant. With the latter, they did not succeed.

The Johnston's were a farm family that lived on the edge of Frankton. Carrie Anne had three older brothers and three older sisters, but they were grown and had left home for work, or college, and, for some, for new families of their own. Carrie Anne was the Johnston's last child of their married life. She had the run of the farm, and, save for her regular visits from Billy, she spent most days playing, or with her mother, helping to take care of the farm animals that were close to home, or cleaning house, or helping in the preparing of meals. What schooling she got, she got from her mother.

The day it happened, Carrie Anne was in the barn, doing nothing more than sitting in the hay, playing with her dolls. Pete Williams and Jake Summers found their way to her. Pete and Jake were local sixteen-year old boys who, up until that day of June 4, 1966, had not been in any trouble worse than being caught smoking and drinking, and getting into fights at school. On that day in June, they got into the worst trouble that they would ever know.

Pete Williams and Jake Summers raped Carrie Anne Johnston. They did it, as near as anyone knows, because they wanted to, and because they thought they could do it without getting caught. They were wrong about not getting caught, and it turned out to be the last mistake in judgment of their short lives. Billy caught them.

Billy came upon them in the barn after Pete had finished and was putting on his pants, and Jake was pushing himself back and forth inside Carrie Anne. Billy pulled Jake off Carrie Anne, twisted his head and broke his neck, and threw his dead body onto the hay covered wooden floor of the Johnston's barn. Pete then tried to run away. Billy grabbed him, twisted his head and broke his neck, and threw his dead body next to Jake's. Billy then pulled Carrie Anne's skirt back down over her legs and sat down beside her. That's how Carrie Anne's mother found them when she came in the barn a few minutes later, looking for Carrie Anne.

The county attorney, Dan Jenkins, charged Billy with manslaughter. Pete Williams and Jake Summer's parents wanted a murder charge. To Carrie Anne's parents, Billy was a hero. The town of Frankton was divided. On the one hand, no one disagreed that what Pete Williams and Jake Summers had done was wrong. On the other hand, a lot of people thought Billy had gone too far in killing the boys. No one quite understood why Billy had done that. No one in Frankton had ever seen Billy act like he would harm anyone.

In the end, it was decided, through the Frankton County District Court, that Billy could not be held responsible for committing a crime. Billy was sent for treatment to the state hospital in Larned, where he remained for a year, before being returned to the custody of his parents in Frankton. This satisfied most of the people of Frankton. It did not satisfy Pete William's and Jake Summer's parents.

V.

Carrie Anne missed her next period following the rape, and a subsequent visit to Doc Taylor confirmed that she was pregnant. It was assumed the father of the unborn child had been either Pete Williams or Jake Summers.

Doc Taylor wanted to abort the pregnancy, even though he was not certain an abortion would be legal. Rape was not a legal reason for abortion in Kansas in 1966. Legal or not, it did not matter to Carrie Anne's parents. The Johnston's would not approve an abortion, notwithstanding Doc Taylor's concerns that delivery might be dangerous for Carrie Anne.

A baby boy was subsequently born to Carrie Anne. The boy was born healthy. Carrie Anne died during delivery.

The Johnston's mourned the death of their daughter, but the Johnston's had known that Carrie Anne might die. The Johnston's faith was strong. They turned their attention to the practical task of raising their grandson. Neither set of parents of the dead boys laid claim to a grandson born of a retarded girl upon whom they laid part of the blame for the death of their sons. The Johnston's adopted the boy as their own. They named him William Francis Johnston, to honor Billy. They called him Frankie.

The Johnston's, and Doc Taylor, watched Frankie close. They watched him to see whether Frankie showed any signs of being retarded like Carrie Anne. But Frankie showed no signs of delayed development or retardation. His first year of life was that of a normal child. He was a blond headed boy. He had his mother's fair hair and fair skin. And, by the time he was one year of age, he had magnificent eyes, the color of coral reef waters of turquoise sea blue.

Charlie

A Memoir Poem

He'd never been to school. They didn't send kids like him to school in the 1920's. He couldn't read. He couldn't write. His face always looked like he knew something funny that you didn't. He was "a little slow." The educated word that would come to be said was "retarded." Now it's "intellectually impaired", or something like that. He wasn't a kid anymore when I knew him. He was a man. I can't tell you how old. I only remember seeing him once. He was kind to me. He liked to take the cork out of Coke bottle caps and put the cap on the outside of your shirt, and the cork on the inside to make a button. I never knew what went on inside his head. What kind of life he lived. He's dead now. We walked down a dusty Arkansas road one summer day when I was a boy, and he made a button out of a bottle cap for me. That's all I remember. Maybe his life was okay. Okay to him I mean. I don't know. I think he should have had something more. I think that now. I didn't know any better then. He was my mother's Great Aunt Donie's stepchild, by reason of her marriage to her second husband, and his name was Charlie.

Kemosabe

A Memoir Poem

When I was a boy, my brother Steve and I sent off for Lone Ranger masks and silver bullets. Steve, Stephen Clay, is twenty-one months younger than me. Sometime between the ages of five and seven, before the age of reason, and at about the same time we were sending off for Lone Ranger masks and silver bullets, Steve was giving sermons. He would mount an overturned washtub, or a back porch step, or an old tree stump, and preach like a Baptist minister. Steve had hearing loss from birth, which I think was part of what made it a little harder for him to find his voice. I understand now what I did not understand then. I was too busy being shy myself. Children are never perfect. Parents are never perfect. Voices get distorted. Voices get lost. Voices are never fully found.

Steve and I each got twenty-five cents a week from dad as allowance to help mom out with chores around the house – which is not to say we could have refused to do the chores if we had not gotten the allowance. We sent in fifteen cents each and two "clue slips" each for our Lone Ranger masks and silver bullets. One clue slip was in every specially marked box of the General Mills cereal – we liked Wheaties and Cheerios best – that we (our mom) had to buy. Mom, I think, was twenty-six years old. The clue was about how the Lone Ranger – *who was that masked man?* – and Tonto caught outlaws. The mail went out and we waited and the mail came back and our prizes were revealed. Steve and I were proud of our masks and our silver bullets, and the deputy badges and identification cards that came with them. We watched the Lone Ranger and Tonto through our masks, on the black and white blonde boxed Sylvania, as we sat cross legged on the floor in our shorts, eating our cereal, before we got dressed and did our Saturday chores.

The Revelation of the Rose

Love lays the heart open
like a cut red rose at its fullest bloom.
But love is not the only passion of the heart.
And some roses never bloom enough for love.
Yet all passion reveals the heart.
And like the revelation of the rose,
the heart blooms enough to die.

Section IV

DIFFERENCE AND LOVE AND RACE

The Snot-Nosed Kid

We were all eight years old in that fall of our childhoods. We got together every Saturday for a couple of hours of football at the playground in the south part of town. I wasn't much of a football player, but boyhood sometimes has obligations, and being part of the Saturday football game was one of them.

There was Jimmy Jackson. His dad ran the local hardware store. Tommy Masters was there. His dad worked for the local highway department. His mom worked at a local flower shop. And Larry Simms. His dad was the local chief of police. Randy Fredrick's dad ran a local grocery store. And Buddy Wilson. His dad had the Ford dealership. Mickey Wiggins was a regular. His dad owned a local bar and restaurant. And Marty Miller, son of the owner of the local John Deere dealership. And me, Chet Fuller, a preacher's kid. Eight of us. Four on a team. One to pass or run. One to hike, block, and go out for passes. The other two to block and take pitches or go out for passes. The four opponents defended.

It wasn't complicated. We switched around every Saturday as to who would be captains, and then we flipped a coin to see who would get to make first choice on dividing up teams. We got to the playground on our bikes around eleven and played till around one. The days were mild. Fallen leaves were blown and scattered over the patch of grass we used for a field. Dressed in sweatshirts and jeans we were grass stained and sweaty by the time one o'clock came around. Some of us were a little bruised and bloodied, too.

This was 1958. Girls didn't exist for us yet. Unless we had sisters, in which case they really didn't exist for us. Our world revolved around the seasons of sport. Football in the fall, basketball in the winter, track in the spring, and baseball in the summer. In between all that was school we had to attend, movies we could go to when our parents gave us the money to go, and TV.

Some of us had more money than others. Mickey Wiggins always had some money in his pockets. I thought at the time it was because his dad made a lot of money out of running the "Frankton Bar and Grill" – Frankton being the name of our little town in the flatland farm country of the Kansas Midwest. Truth was, while Jake Wiggins did make a good living out of selling beers and steaks to folks in town, it was really Marty Miller's dad who was raking in the dough, relatively speaking. Farm implements were cheaper than they are now, but still, we were in farm country and combines and tractors sold. More importantly, even though the Miller's lived in town, Marty's dad owned a farm. Marty never had a lot of money in his pockets though. We thought his dad was just tight with a dollar, or maybe the fact that Marty had six sisters and a brother made things spread a little thin. Marty was a member of a practicing Catholic family. Me, I was the local Baptist preacher's kid, an only child, and I never had any money in my pockets. Baptist preachers in small towns in Kansas never got rich – then or now.

And then there was the race thing. Tommy Masters, whose dad had a government job with the local branch of the state highway department, was black. Except, most people didn't say black back in those days. The polite word then was "colored." Nigger was what was spoken in more casual moments. This kind of distinction filtered down to all of us eight-year olds from our dads and moms, mainly dads. They were not enlightened days. The good part was that when we were all together on that patch of playground football field we really didn't care much about that shit. Shit that was way beyond our control anyway. We tried to play what we thought was football in the best way we knew how at the time. And Tommy was pretty good at football. Not the best of us at the game, but pretty good. The shit of racism came out sometimes, but we were mostly able to keep it from spoiling our fun. I said mostly.

The most racist kid amongst us, and the best football player, and the toughest kid, was Marty Miller. We called Marty (not to his face) the snot-nosed kid. When he was about half an hour into our Saturday games you could see the snot coming out of his nose. By that time a little blood might be coming out of that nose, too. Bruises the size of walnuts could be found on his arms and sides, and they had to also be on his thighs and lower legs. Bruises that changed from red, to blue, to green, to walnut brown, over the course of our fall football Saturdays. Not that the rest of us didn't get a little banged up, too. But Marty seemed to like it the most. (I liked it the least.) It seemed that Marty didn't think the game was worth playing unless snot was exiting his nostrils, and he was acquiring some new bruises, and he had a little blood on his jeans. He wanted to get some of his snot and blood on you, too. And he wanted you to bleed.

One Saturday that fall we were having our usual Saturday game. We were about an hour into the game, about halfway done, with Marty's team leading, as was usually the case, when Marty and Tommy had a run in. Marty had taken the hike from me and took off running around the left end. Marty was a good passer, the best amongst us, and also the fastest runner amongst us. The only one of us who came as close to being as fast was Tommy. This time, Marty got kind of a slow start around the end, and Tommy cut him off before he reached the goal line at the south end of the field. Tommy cut him off hard. He hit him with his head and forearms in Marty's gut, and Marty caved to the ground with Tommy on top of him.

Marty pushed back against Tommy yelling, "Get off me, nig!"

Marty was, as usual, sporting a snout full of snot with a little blood. Marty could take a hit, even liked it to a certain extent, that's why he was such a good football player. And, even as fast as he was, with the good moves he had, he got hit once in awhile. Otherwise, why play the game? So this wasn't the first time he had got hit, and even though we all knew, that is, all of us white kids knew, based upon what Marty let slip when Tommy wasn't around, of Marty's dislike and discomfort with Tommy's blackness, this was the first time we had heard Marty come at Tommy directly with a bad word about that blackness. So, we were surprised.

Tommy got up. Some of Marty's blood and snot were smeared over his navy blue sweat shirt. "What'd you call me?" he asked.

"I said nig," Marty said.

"Don't call me that," Tommy said.

"I will if I want," Marty said.

Mickey spoke up.

"That's enough," Mickey said. "He tackled you fair and square, Marty."

Marty said nothing but gave Mickey a bad look and yelled at me, and Larry, and Randy. "Huddle up!" We did, and Tommy, and Buddy, and Jimmy, and Mickey got ready for the next play. Tommy said nothing more. On the next play, Marty ran it again and scored.

After the game that Saturday, like we did most Saturdays, all of us went over to Mrs. Miller's house, about a block away from the playground, for some baloney sandwiches and chocolate chip cookies. We washed them down with Kool-Aid. Mrs. Miller made great chocolate chip cookies—big, warm cookies, with warm, wet drops of chocolate. I say all of us went, but Tommy didn't go that Saturday. He went home. When Mrs. Miller asked why, we just said that his mom had something for him to do and he couldn't stay.

Usually, when we were at the Miller's, some of Marty's sisters or his brother Mitch would be around. Mitch was the oldest. He was seventeen and in his senior year in high school. Mitch was a starting linebacker on the high school football team. He led the team in tackles. Marty looked up to him a lot. Mitch was home that Saturday, because we all saw him pass by the kitchen as we came in the back door. But he didn't come in and say hi. I thought that was a little unusual, because Mitch usually liked to come in and show off in front of his younger brother's friends. Marty seemed to like that, too. However, Mitch had been hurt in a game a couple of weeks before, and hadn't played since, so I figured maybe he was just not feeling all that well and was just keeping to himself. Mrs. Miller wasn't her usual cheery self, either. She was usually talking a lot and asking us how each of us were doing, and about our parents, and giving us hugs despite our resistance. That morning she was mostly quiet and said, "Enjoy your cookies, boys" and left. We all found out why from our respective parents, later that week. There were no more Saturday football games that fall.

Mitch had brain cancer. He got helmeted in the head in the game against Jefferson, a couple of weeks before that last Saturday when we were all over at the Millers. They did some tests and found the cancer. He had been taken out of the game after the hit feeling dizzy. Everyone thought that it was just a concussion. I say "just a concussion" meaning the kind that didn't cause serious injury. Turns out, he did have a concussion and it wasn't the serious kind but they found the cancer, too.

The Millers had gotten the news of the diagnosis that Friday before the Saturday of our regular football game. The rest of us got the news from our parents later the next week. The Millers knew it was bad, of course. Brain cancer was never good.

Mitch died in the spring. The radiation treatments, the chemotherapy, and what surgery the doctors could do kept him alive through the winter. The funeral was after Easter, the first Saturday in May. Our football group had seen each other in school and on other occasions during this time. But we had talked little about Mitch. We didn't know how. Marty never brought it up.

The day of the funeral it was sunny. No clouds. A little Kansas wind.

All of us went to the funeral with our parents. My dad told me to expect a different sort of funeral service than the one I had been to when my grandmother died. It was a Catholic church. Parts of the service were in Latin. But, it was sad. No difference there. They had an open casket and we all walked by. There were flowers all around the casket. Most of them delivered by Tommy's mom. I didn't understand open caskets then, and I don't now. Mitch didn't look like Mitch. His face looked like it was made of wax.

Marty was sitting with his parents and his sisters. And he was crying. Not surprising for a funeral, but I had never seen Marty cry. His face was red and wet. He had a white handkerchief which he kept bringing up to wipe his nose.

After the service we all went to the Frankton Cemetery for the burial. The cemetery was not far from the Miller's home, and not far from the park where we played football. When we got to the cemetery, we boys stood together in back of the Miller family, Mitch's friends, our parents, and other grown-ups who were standing around what would be Mitch's grave. We were all dressed in white shirts with dark ties and dark sport coats. I kept pulling at my collar trying to loosen the tightness of the tie my dad had knotted around my neck. I wasn't the only one.

After they lowered Mitch into the ground, and the priest had said a few words about how great Mitch was and how he would now be in Heaven where he would have no more pain, Marty came around to where we were all standing. His face was still red and wet. He said, "Thanks for comin." And each of us said something like, "Sure, Marty." Then Marty jumped Tommy.

Marty was on top of Tommy pounding him as hard as he could with his fists. He was pounding him in the face and in his chest and in his stomach. All over. No real plan to his fists. They were just pounding Tommy hard. And all the while Marty was crying, and his face was getting even redder, and he was dripping snot all over Tommy. Tommy was doing his best to use his arms to keep Tommy's fists off of him, but a lot of the blows were landing. The grown-ups had noticed what was going on, and I could see them moving towards us. Mickey and I got to Marty before the grown-ups got to us, and pulled him off Tommy just long enough for Tommy to get up and get away from us.

"Stop it, Marty!" we yelled. "Stop it!"

And then all of a sudden, Marty did stop it. And he fell to the ground and he was breathing deep like he needed air. He lay there, just heaving and crying, till Mr. Miller came and picked him up and carried him away. By this time, Tommy's parents had also come to where we were, and they were leading Tommy away to their car. Tommy wasn't crying, but he was bent over, and his face and clothes were bloody.

My mom and dad said that Marty was obviously upset about his brother's death and lost control of himself in his grief. From what the other boys told me, excepting for Tommy, who didn't talk about it, that's pretty much what their parents told them. If Tommy was mad he didn't show it at school or when I saw him during that summer, and I never heard about Mr. and Mrs. Masters doing anything about what happened. Before school started next fall, Tommy's Dad got a job with another highway office and they moved to Topeka, which I thought would have been a big change from Frankton.

After that, I never saw Tommy again. Ten years later he died from a sniper's bullet in Vietnam. The rest of us stayed in Frankton and graduated high school. Jimmy Jackson went on to become an engineer. Larry Simms became a police officer like his dad. Randy Fredricks got a business degree and went to work for an insurance company. Mickey took over his dad's bar and grill. Buddy moved to Kansas City, and was a manager in the Ford plant there. Marty became a priest and eventually moved to Oklahoma City.

Me, I was a high school English teacher in St. Paul, Minnesota until I retired in 2008. I have told you about what happened because I was the one best able to do it, and because I thought it was a story that needed to be told. That is all I can tell you. I have found no ending for the problem of difference or the pain of being human.

Across the Years

Sophia and John are laughing.
They are not laughing for you,
but their laughing is a gift.
Sophia and John have black hair.
Like their father.
Like their mother -
who left their father.
Their eyes?
You try not to get too close.
Old men have to be careful.
But you have seen.
They are the color of coffee.
Their skin is coffee creamed.
Two children from down the block
who wave hello and goodbye
as you come and you go.
A tire is swinging.
Swinging by a rope from an oak tree.
Swinging like the tongue of a clock -
if time could be uncertain.
Sophia is pushing John.
John is swinging with Sophia's push.
They call your name -
across the years.
You call their names -
across the years.
They will forget you -
across the years.

Children of the Sun

I see the graves of my grandchildren.
The bones of the children of my children
buried in the land.
The dead bones of black
and white and brown and crimson
and golden
children of the sun.

The graves of my grandchildren call out to me.
Let nothing spoil the memory of them.
A memory I will never know.
Multitudes came before
and have come and will come after.

I who never fathered a child.
I dream their dreams.
I hear their cries in the night.
I see them
girls and boys
dying young and old.

Hair that was sometimes
a purple or an orange
or a green.
Skins tattooed blue.
Bodies pierced with silver
and gold.

Your fathers and
your mothers –
not always understanding
sometimes forgetting –
the vagaries of youth.

You will disappear
as those who have
disappeared before you.
As will those who
come after you.

Children of the sun
I worship you.

Dreamdust

"Stardust is
the hardest thing
to hold out for."

from *Stardust*
by Kay Ryan

Dust, Dreamdust, Stardust:
The hardest part is the human part.

The Whole Truth

The truth is always partial.

Section V

DIFFERENCE AND LOVE AND WAR

My Conversation with Max

I.

The year was 1974 and I was twenty-four. I was the night shift manager at the 7/11 store on South U.S. Highway 59 in Lawrence, Kansas. I had graduated from the university a couple of years back, and I was going to move to Topeka in late August to start law school. Max was sixty years old. He was a small man. Ninety to a hundred pounds. About five foot four or five. He didn't have much hair left, and what he did have left was usually spread uncombed in long grey strands against his otherwise bald head. I worked at that 7/11 from January through July of 1974, and I always remember Max being dressed the same. In cold weather, he wore one of those all-purpose, lightweight poly-cotton men's overcoats (with the zip-in fake fur liner removed), a light grey in color, cut to just above the knee. He wore it open. Underneath he wore a dingy white shirt and grey or navy blue dress pants. He wore a black leather belt, cinched tight, and he wore black dress shoes, unshined. In warm weather, he took the overcoat off. Otherwise, there was no change.

Max was an old white guy, but he chain-smoked Kool's. His teeth looked like they had been brushed with dirty brown water, that didn't rinse, a result of years—in Max's case decades—of cigarette smoke passing over and through them on its way to Max's lungs. Lungs which undoubtedly looked like they had been washed in dirty brown water too, if you could have seen them. His fingers were tobacco-stained brown on both hands at the fingertips. Fingertips finished off in nails that needed clipping.

No one else who worked at the store liked Max. In addition to not liking how he looked, they didn't like that Max would come into the store and buy a pack of Kool's and a bottle of Maalox, then smoke one and drink the other while hanging around the store. He didn't go away soon enough for them. Max had ulcers, bad digestion, and heartburn. He also liked to drink. I never saw Max act in a way that made me think he was drunk, but I did see him chase vodka out of a bottle with Maalox out of a bottle more than once.

Max was a lawyer. A Jewish lawyer. But he was not a rich Jewish lawyer. Not anymore. He had drunk it all up. His wife had left him over the drinking. He never saw her. He had a daughter about my age living somewhere out in California. He told me once he called her regularly, but she never called him. She hadn't gotten over how his drinking had hurt her mother and used up all their money. All of Max's other relation had died during World War II, at Dachau.

Max usually wanted to talk. I talked back. I felt sorry for Max. He was old (well, he seemed old to me at the time) and he was lonely, and no one liked him. I was trying to be nice. But it was more than being nice or feeling sorry for him. Max was a challenge.

Max said he had been an intelligence officer in the Army during World War II. He told me he thought I would have made a good staff officer.

II.

"It was the wrong thing to do, Max."

"We had no choice, Johnny."

"Of course we had a choice. People always have a choice. You do believe in free will, don't you, Max?"

"You weren't there, Johnny. You don't understand. You don't understand the mood of the country."

"Look Max, you're right, I wasn't there. But, that doesn't mean I don't understand the difference between right and wrong. Two thirds of the Japanese that we locked up were American citizens. There were Japanese Americans who fought in World War II, for Christ's sake. It was the wrong thing to do."

"Pearl Harbor, Johnny, Pearl Harbor."

"That was done by the enemy, Max. That wasn't done by U.S. citizens, which is who the Japanese Americans were that we locked up."

"You keep saying locked up, Johnny. They were put in relocation camps, not in prison."

"Jesus, Max, they were put in camps behind barbed wire fences and they weren't allowed to leave. It sounds like a fucking prison to me. I think you would have thought so if you'd been there."

"Okay, okay. But, you still don't understand. They may have been Americans, but they were Japanese Americans. We couldn't take the chance. Not after Pearl Harbor. We couldn't take the chance that there might not be enemies living right here. We had to separate them out. There might have been spies among them. They were still Japanese. They had ties to the homeland. Besides, it was for their good, too, Johnny. People in the country were angry. Separating them out was also for their protection."

"I've never read anything anywhere that, even if there was some argument to be made that it was in part for their protection, that would have justified taking away their homes and locking them up in camps behind barbed wire. They locked up whole families, dammit. Are you saying that we would have done the same thing if say, the Irish had attacked Pearl Harbor?"

"Don't be silly, Johnny. And it would have been really cruel not to have kept the families together."

"I'm not being silly, Max. The reason we locked them up was because we could. And the reason we could is because they didn't look like us. It was racist. It was bigoted. It was wrong."

"The fact that they looked different than us, and because of that it made it easier to identify them, doesn't make what we did wrong, Johnny. And it doesn't make it racist or bigoted. I think I know a little more about bigotry than you do, Johnny. They looked like the enemy. Some of them could have been spying for the enemy. We were at war. We had been attacked. We had to do what was best for the country."

"Listen to yourself, Max. You're saying them and us. They were part of the country, Max. They were part of the country."

"It's easy for you to say things like that now, Johnny. We're standing here, smoking cigarettes, having a conversation. We're not afraid, Johnny. We're not afraid."

"Fear doesn't justify everything, Max."

"Maybe not, Johnny. But, it's easy to look back and say something was wrong, when nothing bad happened. What if there had been spies among those Japanese? And, what if they had been able to get information that led to bombing inside this country, for instance? If that had happened, what we did would now look like it had made a whole lot of sense. The only problem would be that we didn't do a good enough job of it."

"You're better at history than I am, Max. But, for all I know, there may have been spies among them. If so, that would have made the spies the enemy. It would have been treason. A capital offense. But that doesn't justify taking the homes of people who are not spies, and locking them up behind barbed wire. This is the United States of America, goddammit! This is a free country. We believe in individual rights. We're not some communist country, or some other kind of country with a dictator, that just locks people up who have done nothing wrong, just to keep the dictators in power."

"Sometimes, in times of war, you have to do things that you wouldn't do in other times, Johnny. Otherwise, you might not have a free country anymore. We weren't doing it to keep a dictator in power. We were doing it for us, Johnny, for us. For Americans—for all Americans—including Japanese Americans. To win the war and keep the country safe. So we could keep living the free life."

"The end justifies the means. That's what you're saying, Max? Right? The end justifies the means?"

"Sometimes it does, Johnny. Sometimes it does."

"Torture, Max?"

"We didn't torture the Japanese, Johnny."

"Well, Max, leaving aside that some—not the least of which would be Japanese Americans—might consider what we did to Japanese Americans in World War II as torture, you're not answering my question. There is such a thing as torture—I don't think you're going to disagree with that—is torture a means that would justify an end?"

"That depends on the end, Johnny."

"Well, I guess that's a helluva lot easier to say if you're not part of the means to that end, Max."

"Just because it's easier to say, doesn't mean it's wrong, Johnny. I'm a realist."

"You're saying I'm not a realist?"

"You're an idealist, Johnny. You're an idealist now. You would have been a realist then."

"There were those then who disagreed with what was done to the Japanese Americans, Max."

"And they were wrong, Johnny. They were wrong."

As Max and I spoke he moved around the space between the checkout counter and the aisles to my right in the store. The store was lit by overhead neon lights, so bright and artificial that the dark reality outside, if you could get far enough away from the neon lit parking lot, was deeply missed. I stood most of the time, facing Max, smoking Marlboros, wearing my orange and white checked poly-cotton 7/11 shirt. Customers came and went. Max and I talked in between.

"So, what about the bomb, Max?"

"You mean the bomb dropped on Hiroshima?"

"And Nagasaki."

"It was either them or us, Johnny. And none of them were Japanese Americans."

"But they were women and children, Max, little babies, and old people. They were not using weapons against us. They were civilians."

"Their government went to war with us, Johnny. Pearl Harbor. Japanese soldiers killed our men, killed them viciously, the bastards, and they wouldn't quit. If they would have quit, we wouldn't have had to use the bomb. It was either use the bomb or a lot more of our soldiers were going to die. Soldiers who had wives and children waiting for them to come home."

"But the children in Hiroshima and Nagasaki had no say in what the Japanese government did, Max. Children can't really have a government. They had no say in whether Japanese soldiers quit fighting or not."

"If you want me to say it wasn't fair to those children, you're right, Johnny, it wasn't fair to those children. But, life isn't always fair. Like I said, it was either them or us, and our soldiers had children, too."

"But couldn't we have dropped a bomb to show them what it would be like?"

"We tried to warn them, Johnny. Their leaders wouldn't listen. We only had so many bombs. We couldn't risk waiting."

"We didn't tell them we had the bomb, Max. Not before Hiroshima."

"We tried to get them to surrender, Johnny. They wouldn't. We couldn't risk using a bomb, or letting them know what we had. They wouldn't have believed us anyway. We only had so many bombs."

"So, because some of our soldiers might die, hundreds of thousands of Japanese children had to die horrible deaths or become horribly disabled?"

"A lot of our soldiers, not just some, were going to die if we didn't drop those bombs, Johnny. We couldn't even get them to surrender until after we dropped the second bomb."

"The end justified the means?"

"The end justified the means, Johnny."

"What if we'd had to kill a million little babies, Max? A million little Japanese babies to save a hundred thousand American soldiers? I want to know what, if any, is the limit to your end justifies the means, Max? For that matter, why not sacrifice a million little Japanese babies to save one American soldier? The one American soldier is just as innocent as the hundred thousand isn't he, Max?"

"Well, Johnny, we could turn it around and I could ask you where is the justice for the individual soldier, the individual that you wanted to talk so much about when we were talking about separating out Japanese Americans into camps. Where's the justice for this innocent American soldier? Are you saying it's okay to sacrifice him in order to save the lives of a million Japanese babies? Are you now saying it's okay to sacrifice a few to save the many? Which is what I was saying about sacrificing the rights of Japanese Americans by putting them into camps, for the greater good of all Americans."

"I never accepted that there was a need to separate out Japanese Americans. And anyway, it's a matter of who has the power to decide. Japanese Americans who were put in prison camps weren't deciding to make a sacrifice for the many. That choice was not given to them. The American soldier was already in the position, either because he enlisted or he was drafted, as a requirement of American law, of risking his life for the greater good. True, it was for the greater good of his fellow American citizens, but still, he agreed to take a risk. I don't see that killing an innocent child is justified as a way of removing him from that risk, just because that child is from another country."

"There's no way to keep innocent people from dying in a war, Johnny. We dropped a whole lot of regular bombs in World War II, too. And in Korea. And we've dropped a lot of bombs in Vietnam. And, I expect we'll drop a lot of bombs in whatever war comes next. You can't drop bombs, or shoot at other people, without innocent people sometimes getting killed. The only way to keep innocent people from getting killed in a war, Johnny, is not to have the war in the first place. We haven't figured out a way not to have wars. And Johnny, like I said before, deciding what the right thing is to do is a whole lot different when you're in the situation where the decision has to be made, than it is standing around talking about it outside of that situation. You had to be there. We did what we had to do, as bad as that was."

"There were no military targets in Hiroshima and Nagasaki, were there Max? No primary targets, anyway. The primary targets were the civilians. Wasn't that the point, Max? Wasn't that the fucking point?"

"It had to be done, Johnny. It had to be done."

III.

On July 5th the store was robbed. July 4th was usually a big sales day for the store. This July 4th was no exception. When I took over the shift at midnight, Sandy, the swing shift manager, told me that she and Cory had a busy evening. Things had slowed down some, but she said for me not to be surprised if it picked up a little later. She apologized for not being able to stay and help. There was a lot of re-stocking of the shelves to be done, which they hadn't had time to do earlier. The babysitter could only stay till 1 am, so she had to get home to watch Tina. Danny, her husband, was on a trucking run. Cory refused to stay. He had a party to go to. She said my usual help, Jimmy, had called in sick. I thought at the time, Christ, it was the fucking Fourth of July. She should have made Cory stay. But I said nothing. Sandy knew I would say nothing.

"See you this morning when I get off?"

"Okay," Sandy said.

It was about 4 am when it happened. As it turned out, it hadn't been that busy a night. I was back in the northeast corner of the store, restocking the potato chips. Max was the only other person in the store. He was up front next to the checkout area, smoking. The whole thing probably took only about five, maybe ten minutes, at the most.

I heard the buzzer bell ring, like it did every time a customer came through the front door in the store, and I got up from my knees to see who had come in, and to move to the checkout area. I saw a man, a black man, with one of those winter season black stocking caps with cutouts for the eyes, nose, and mouth, standing by the check-out counter with a gun pointed at Max. His face was covered, but he was wearing a white tee shirt and he had no gloves on. I was no expert on guns, but the cops told me later that it was a nine millimeter semi-automatic. As soon as I stood up, the guy saw me.

He kept pointing the gun at Max and yelled at me, "Open the safe!"

I was sweating. I moved toward the checkout area. I was having a hard time swallowing because I couldn't get any new spit in my mouth. I looked at Max, but he wasn't looking at me. He was looking right back at the guy holding the gun.

I told the guy I didn't have a key for the safe. I thought he was going to shoot me, but he threw me a bag he was holding in his left hand.

"Put everything in the drawer in the bag." All the while, he kept the gun on Max. I could see now that the hand holding the gun was shaking.

I did what he said. I held the bag out back across the counter to him. He took it, and then he started backing out the front door, moving the gun back and forth at Max and me. He didn't say anything else.

I could see a car parked outside facing the store. I could see someone, a man I thought, sitting behind the wheel. Once the guy cleared the front door, he kept backing up towards the passenger side. As soon as he reached it, he opened it and got inside, keeping the gun pointed towards the store all the time. I thought, it's over. They're going to drive away, and I'm going to call the cops. We didn't get hurt. He didn't put us in the cooler and kill us. It's going to be over. It's going to be alright.

Then Max did something I didn't expect and made no sense. Max went out the front door towards the guy. Max had no gun. Max had no weapon of any kind. What the fuck did Max think he was doing for Christ sakes?

By the time Max reached the car, the guy was in the passenger seat and the car had backed up, and they were getting ready to floorboard it out of the parking lot. Which they did. But not before the guy with the gun opened up on Max. I could hear the shots. I don't know how many. But, bam, bam, bam, bam. Then they were gone.

I ran out the front door to where Max was lying. Of the multiple shots the guy had opened up on Max, most had hit Max's face. It was hard to tell it was Max's face any more. Blood was coming out of Max's head. Little pieces of Max's face were mixed with blood and scattered around his head in the asphalt parking lot. I felt the humid warmth of the air. I breathed the humid warmth of the air. I heard the bugs zapping their lives out on the bug lights in front of the store. I turned around and I moved away from Max and I threw up. Then I went inside and called the cops and the store manager.

The cops, and the store manager, let me go home at about seven. Except that I didn't go home. I went to Sandy's. When I got next to her that morning

I didn't say anything. It was all about me. I wanted to take, and I took, and I took, and I took. When I was done I rolled off of her.

"Jesus Christ, Johnny."

Then I told her what had happened. Then I went and bought a fifth of Jack Daniels. Then I went home and got as drunk as I could. Then I threw up. Then I slept.

IV.

They caught them about a week later. It wasn't hard. Their mother turned them in. She overheard them talking about what they had done. The oldest kid, the kid who had the gun and killed Max, was eighteen. His younger brother, the driver, was sixteen. According to what was printed in the Lawrence Journal World, they'd both been drinking that night and the older brother talked the younger brother into the robbery. The eighteen-year old had no prior arrests or convictions. Whether they had juvenile records, the paper had no way of knowing. They had been in some fights at school, according to school sources the paper wouldn't identify. They lived with their mother who was a cafeteria cook at Lawrence High School.

They both pled. The eighteen-year old who killed Max got life with no chance for parole. The sixteen-year old, the younger brother driver, was adjudicated up to an adult. He got life with a chance for parole after doing a minimum of fifteen. I later talked to one of the cops who had been on the case and he told me that if there had been no killing, the eighteen-year old probably would have gotten ten to fifteen for armed robbery with a chance for parole. He also said the district attorney probably would not have gotten the sixteen-year old adjudicated as an adult, but would have left him in juvenile court where he probably would have been locked up in a juvenile facility until he was eighteen, then released, at which time his record would have been sealed.

It was a couple of weeks after the arrests were made, that I got a call from a guy representing Max's life insurance company. He said he needed to talk to me.

"Why do you want to talk to me?" I asked him.

"There's just some things I need to clear up with you, Mr. Henderson." The guy introduced himself as Harold Taylor of American Lifetime Insurance Company.

We met at the Village Inn Pancake House.

Taylor was a middle-aged white guy; I'd say in his mid-fifties. A lot of grey in the hair. A lot overweight. He was dressed in a navy blue sport coat and tie with grey slacks.

We ordered black coffees and cinnamon rolls and exchanged the usual greetings and comments about the weather, which was hot and humid, and I lit a Marlboro and Taylor asked me, "How well did you know Mr. Altman?"

"I always just knew him as Max. We exchanged last names once. But, I always called him Max."

"So, he was a regular customer?"

"Yeah, Max was a regular. I saw him many times in the store at night when I was working."

"So, you talked to him frequently when he was in the store?"

"Yeah. Max and I usually talked when he was in the store. But, why all these questions about how well I knew Max?"

"I'm getting to that, Mr. Henderson. I've read your statement that you gave the police the night of the robbery. You said, and I don't remember your exact words, but you said that you were surprised by what Mr. Altman, Max, did that night, is that right?"

And then it hit me. I knew what was happening. I knew what Taylor was getting at and I thought he could be right, but I also thought it would be a stretch, and I didn't think the insurance company could make that stretch. I certainly wasn't going to help them.

"Well, I don't remember my exact words either, Mr. Taylor, but I'd just seen a man I knew get killed, so I may not have been in the best shape to be saying what had happened."

"I understand, Mr. Henderson, but I've done many of these investigations for ALI, and we usually find that the police do a pretty good job of taking into account the emotional state of the people giving statements. ALI takes that into account, too. The police report states, as I recall, that the officer taking your statement, a Sergeant Mathews—Melissa Mathews if I remember correctly—felt that you were giving clear responses to her questions. And the one question and answer that I, on behalf of ALI, am interested in, is your answer to Sgt. Mathews when she asked you if you knew why Mr. Altman, Max, went out of the store, unarmed, after the gunmen. You said that you were surprised by what Mr. Altman did."

"Look, Mr. Taylor, what I think I meant by that was that, what with the gunmen leaving the store without having shot Max and myself, I thought we were home free. So, it shook me to see Max going out the door. But, as I think I also said in the statement I gave Sgt. Mathews, Max was an alcoholic. He was a drinker. A heavy drinker. And I think he must have just lost it with what happened, and with him being under the influence of alcohol and all, and that's what caused him to go after that gunmen. It wasn't your usual situation, Mr. Taylor."

"It wasn't usual for you either, Mr. Henderson. But you didn't go chasing, unarmed, after a robber who had a gun. Had you ever seen Mr. Altman, as you say, 'lose it' before?"

"Well, I'd never been through a robbery with him. What's this all about, Mr. Taylor? Max made a stupid mistake going out that door. But it wasn't a usual situation. It was a bad situation. It was an unexpected bad situation. People make mistakes in bad situations. People especially make mistakes in unexpected bad situations, whether they're drunk or sober. Anybody can make a mistake. I could have made a mistake. The robbery was a bad situation. We didn't expect to get robbed. It wasn't Max's fault that he died. Max didn't shoot himself. Max wasn't suicidal."

"You're sure about that?"

"I'm sure. Are you saying you don't believe me?"

"No. I'm not saying that, Mr. Henderson. I, that is, we, ALI, just have to do a thorough investigation when one of our policy holders dies under any kind of unusual circumstances when a policy is recently purchased."

"You mean before you pay out on the policy to the beneficiary."

"That's right, Mr. Henderson."

That was pretty much the end of my conversation with Mr. Taylor. I did wonder how a guy in Max's health could have found an insurance company dumb enough to write him a policy, but I did not bring that up with Mr. Taylor. I did bring up with him that I figured the beneficiary was probably Max's daughter, since Max had told me she was his only living relative, not counting his ex-wife. Mr. Taylor told me he couldn't tell me who the beneficiary was, and I told him I understood that, but, if it was Max's daughter, would he please tell her how to get in touch with me because I would like to tell her that I was sorry about her father's death. He said he could do that.

ALI paid on Max's life insurance. I found this out about a month later when Max's daughter, Sarah, called me. Sarah needed money for a kidney transplant, which she now had, along with some additional VA benefits. Max had wanted to be the donor, too, but he only had one kidney, as a result of losing a kidney to infection during the war. In any case, there had been no money for it yet, and they thought her mother would be a better match. Max's kidney, like his liver, and his lungs, and his other organs probably hadn't been in the best of shape.

V.

I'm not sure whether Max got himself killed on purpose or not. But I can't think of any other reason Max would have done what he did. Max was drinking and smoking himself to death, alright, but that was slow suicide. If, as it turned out, his daughter needed the money right away, then getting himself killed in a robbery was an opportune way to do it. If that's true, it took a lot of balls. I won't say Max was wrong for doing it. Not wrong in so far as getting himself killed. If suicide is a sin, then I'll let any God that's available take care of any punishment Max is due for it. Whether saving his daughter the way he did justified what it did to those boys? I don't know. Whether Max would have thought so? Yeah, I think Max would have thought so.

Collateral Damage

Sometimes mistakes are made.
Sometimes mistakes are not made.
The enemy is sought
where human eyes can also see.

Joe's War

Joe was in the Pacific during the war.
He saw men he knew killed.
He killed men he did not know.

After the war,
Joe worked as a crop duster in the Rio Grande Valley,
and he drank whiskey,
and he tried to forget the war.

Then Joe found the arms of Maria,
and he married Maria,
and he fathered a daughter,
and he fathered a son.

And Joe thought less of the war,
and he drank less whiskey,
and he had a good life.

Then a third child was stillborn,
and Maria grieved,
and Maria took a few too many pills to help her sleep,
and Maria lost her life.

And Joe grieved for Maria,
and Joe drank more whiskey,
and Joe drank until death.

The military buried Joe,
one kill short of a flyboy Ace,
in the spring air of the very next spring –
on Memorial Day,
in Memorial Cemetery,
at the end of Memorial Road –
in the same small space of earth where lay Maria,
the mother of Joe's daughter,
and the mother of Joe's son.

The war was a memory.
Joe's war was a memory.
Joe was a memory.

The Morally Just War

If your death would bring the justice you seek –
Would the justice you seek be worth your death?
If your torture would bring the justice you seek –
Would the justice you seek be worth your torture?

If a child's death would bring the justice you seek –
Would the justice you seek be worth a child's death?
If a child's torture would bring the justice you seek –
Would the justice you seek be worth a child's torture?

And who is not an innocent?
And what is not innocence?
And what innocence is worth war's justice?

If a sinner's death would bring the justice you seek –
Would the justice you seek be worth a sinner's death?
If a sinner's torture would bring the justice you seek –
Would the justice you seek be worth a sinner's torture?

And who is not a sinner?
And what is not a sin?
And what sin is worth war's justice?

Section VI

DEATH

Fertile Ground

I.

It was a good day for plowing. The August sky was clear. The rich, dark, earth met the hard metal that made the furrows. Farmer complaints were of two types – it was either too wet, or too dry. Today, there was no reason for either complaint. Today, a farmer could work.

Jacob Carter was a farmer who worked. The land on which he and Emma had built their home and had raised their three sons and two daughters, was his thanks to his hard work, and Emma's hard work, and the willingness of the bank to take a chance on a farm hand and a school teacher. Jacob and Emma had worked, and saved, and built. The bank had been paid. The children had been raised. Jacob and Emma had prospered.

Jacob had led a religious life. Emma had seen to that. There were no more reliable Baptists than the Carters. They were at church every Sunday, unless they were out of town, or sickness kept them away. Emma had sung in the church choir. Jacob was a deacon and a Sunday school teacher. All five children – Joshua, James, William, Amanda, and the youngest, Emily – had attended, although not without some teenage protest when they came of that age.

II.

Today, a clear and sunny Saturday, and the first day of August, Jacob rode a John Deere across a quarter of his wheat ground, plowing the harvested field, working the ground for the fall planting. When Jacob plowed, he liked doing it on a tractor that let the smell and taste of earth and machine reach him accompanied by the sound of the steady and rapid chug, chug, chug of the John Deere's engine. He had no air conditioned cab. The canvas sunshade that extended above him was his only air conditioner.

The tractor radio was tuned to station KRGI, 96.5, FM country classics, broadcasting out of Grand Island. Jacob listened to voices that expected nothing of him in return.

III.

Jacob had a sermon to prepare. The Baptist preacher and his family, the Reverend James White, and his wife Gloria, and their daughters Suzanne and Beverly, were taking their annual two week vacation. It was the custom for the deacons to provide for Sunday services for the two Sundays that the minister and his family were gone. Jacob had agreed in January to provide the sermon for the first Sunday of Rev. White's absence. After Emma died, the other deacons offered to relieve Jacob of this responsibility. Jacob had thanked them for their kindnesses, but had declined their offers.

Jacob wanted a drink, but he didn't drink. He had a cold bottle of beer now and then, but Emma had allowed that didn't count. He steadied the tractor steering wheel with his left hand and grabbed the hard plastic jug of water behind the seat. He flipped open the plastic tab at the top, brought the jug up to his mouth with his right hand, and took a long, cold drink. He then put the jug back behind the seat, and went with his right hand inside his blue cotton short-sleeve work-shirt pocket, inside his blue denim bib overalls, and found a pack of cigarettes and a plastic lighter. He had started smoking again. He shuffled an Old Gold out of the pack and put his lips around the filter tip. He put the cigarettes back in his pocket, got the lighter, and brought the lighter up and lit the cigarette. He inhaled, and then took the cigarette from his lips and exhaled, holding the lighter in his palm, and then moved the cigarette to his left hand and put the lighter back in his shirt pocket. After a moment of removing the Farmer's Co-op baseball cap he was wearing, and wiping the sweat from his forehead with his forearm, he put two hands back on the tractor steering wheel.

IV.

Jacob moved the tractor through the stubbled wheat field, turning the stubble with the plow, making the ground to be plowed ever less as he did so. There was a hawk circling in the blue sky above. She was a great grey and white bird with a reddish brown tail, riding the hot August air with her feathered wings. Jacob saw her at an angle, losing sight of her when her path took her above the sunshade which was above Jacob. When a hawk circled, a hawk's prey could usually be found on the ground within the boundary of that circle. Jacob's eyes searched the ground around him. His eyes were not as good as the hawk's eyes, but his searching nonetheless succeeded in revealing the hawk's prey. A small light brown and white jackrabbit, long of ear and long of hinged hind legs, was moving under and through the ever decreasing stubble that Jacob's plow was turning under.

The rabbit was trying to avoid the noise and smell of the John Deere's engine, and the shaking of the ground caused by the tractor and the plow. He could do so by moving deeper into the unplowed stubble, but only for so long as the machine's work was unfinished. All of the fields next to the field Jacob was plowing, save one, had been plowed. The field to Jacob's east, across ground Jacob had plowed, was grass to be used for cow pasture. Eventually, the rabbit must either run out of the stubble and onto plowed ground, and within the greater ability of the hawk's eyes, and claws, or he must be plowed under. Jacob had seen rabbits run, and hawks eat. He had seen rabbits run, and hawks go hungry. He had seen a rabbit plowed under.

Jacob remembered the first time. He remembered back sixty-four years. Jacob had trouble remembering short. He could usually better remember long. He had been sixteen-years old. It was another Kansas field in another Kansas place, and Jacob had a summer job plowing. He remembered that summer because a girl named Jessie, the first love of his life before Emma, had broke with him, taking his innocence from heartbreak from him. It was a high school hurt, but it was a hurt. He plowed that field that summer trying to cry, and trying not to cry, and not always succeeding in his trying. He remembered a day with a hawk circling and a rabbit hiding. He plowed the rabbit under. At least, that is how he remembered it.

Jacob kept plowing the field. The rabbit ran over plowed ground. It's not easy to run over plowed ground, even if you're a rabbit. But this rabbit made it to the fence on the east side of the field, and to a bushy hiding place in the grass field on the other side of the fence. The hawk had tried and missed.

V.

Jacob stopped the John Deere next to his truck, next to the gate for the field he had plowed. He shut down the tractor engine and turned the tractor radio off. He lit another Old Gold and smoked it, slowly. The sun was going. He got off the tractor and dropped the remains of the cigarette to the ground and crushed it with the heel of his work boot. He had his sermon.

A Grandson's Story

A Memoir Poem

My grandfather, on my mother's side, was a lineman for the Arkansas Power and Light Company. He had also been a school janitor, and had done farm work, and had worked for the WPA. My grandmother was a housewife for all of her married life, except for the brief time she worked at a munitions plant during the war. After granddad died, grandmother got about six hundred dollars a month in death pension benefits, until the money ran out a few years later. She also worked as a short order cook, and then lived on social security, with help from my parents. She never remarried. Two of her children and two of her grandchildren died before she did. I remember granddad for the times he took me fishing, and for the old grey sweat-stained fedora he wore, and for the bib jean overalls he wore, and for the L&M's he smoked by the carton, packs of which I used to steal. The first time granddad saw me, he was in the hospital. He had touched a broken power line. I was just a baby. My parents' first child and my grandparents' first grandchild. My grandmother told me she took me round to granddad's hospital window and held me up for him to see. My grandmother told me this when she was in her nineties, not long before she died. My granddad had long since been dead by then, dying at the age of fifty-eight. The official cause of granddad's death was a blood disease, but I'm not sure he ever completely recovered from touching the broken power line that put him in the hospital where my grandmother held me up for him to see. Thirty-eight years later, after granddad's death, my grandmother never completely recovered from the cancer that was eating at her body, while she was lying in the Arkansas nursing home bed where I last saw her. Someday, I will not completely recover from something. Only the story will remain.

A Lifetime

Read a life.
Write a life.
Die on time.

A Matter of Time

You try to find a few words.
You try to let a few words find you.
You think of that old picture.
Some sixty-two years now gone by.
You a baby in your father's arms.
Side by side with your mother.
Twenty and nineteen.
Wavy-haired beauties of youth.
Where is the way to make
time and distance specific?
To explain all the conversation lost.
Would silence have been better?
Would silence be better?
In ten thousand million years what will it matter?
It's only been sixty-two years so far,
and no one remembers who took that picture.

A Matter of Words

There are days
of death poems.
Days of memory.
Days of light.
Days where we exist
only in the lonely afterglow
of darkness.
We weep.
We whisper.
We are written
as children.
We were children.
We become children.
There are landscapes
of darkness.
There are landscapes
of light.
We have daydreams.
We have night dreams.
We have dreams
of days and nights.
Ordinary seasons
with silent
whispering skies.
You think of being nothing.
You think of oblivion.
You think of death.
Death can steal away your sorrow.
You will die and leave
the gift of life
behind for others.

You who were so soft
to my touch.
Your sex
melting into eternity.
Vanishing from the shadows.
Childlike.
A poem written too soon.
A poem too short.
A poem now gone.
The wistful whisper of children.

A Thing of Beauty

Death is a perfect thing.
It is a thing complete in itself.
Nothing to add.
Nothing to leave out.
It is a thing of beauty.

Death at Any Age

The sound of children laughing in the summer air.
Outside my window laughing where no one knows a care.
No disease, no death, no heartbreak, no tears for me to hear.
What tricks God plays on us, just to catch us unawares.

In old age, if we are so lucky, we know what pain awaits.
The joys we have today, tomorrows wait to break.
We could not tell the children, even if we were so cruel.
They would not understand us, their lives are full of school.

Nursery rhymes and playground games tease their lives along.
Sadder times lie ahead in the death of friends and funeral songs.
Death that comes to friends once young but also friends now gone.
Unless of course they died in youth, God's greatest gift gone wrong.

Perhaps this is the way God planned it with silly poetry -
Childhood dreams turn grey in a world made real with human misery -
Sweet joys he grants along life's way must end in darkness and eternity -
Perhaps this is the way God planned it, but damn him anyway.

Death Words

Death by cold
Death by fire
Death by air
Death by water
Death rising
Death descending
Death tragic
Death heroic
Death singing
Death crying
Death light
Death dark
Death soulful
Death soulless
Death lost
Death found
Death silent
Death loud
Death humble
Death proud
Death real
Death romantic
Death prosaic
Death poetic
Death remembered
Death forgotten
Death ending
Death beginning

Empty Spaces

The love letters lay shoe boxed.
The books were on the shelves.
The books were on the tables.
The books were by the bed.

The electronic screen held a history.
Where there were words he had searched -
Where there were words he had written -
Where there were words he had not found.

I remembered how he moved through time -
Once young, then old, then older still.
I remembered how he moved through space -
Quicker, then slower, then slower still.

I remember him now.
I shall remember him till I am memory.
I shall remember him till I leave him.
I shall remember him till I am gone.

Freedom

The stories he told will be told no more.
Some light has disappeared out of light
and into the darkness eternal.
Where all stories go, so he has gone.
The moon shines on
but even the moon –
that reflected light
from the fire of life -
like the fire of life -
is not eternal.
We are told these days
that stories are the problem.
Stories are the prisons
from which we must escape.
But we are also told that
there is no we
no I
no me
no self.
We are trapped
but we are not really here.
It is all true of course
and it is all a lie.
A story must live
before a story can die.

Gravesong

The triumphs of who we think we are
are but brief reflections of our lights
in the darkness of our short times.
The darkness was here before
and will be here after
we have flickered away.
Darkness is the birthright of the rich and the poor.
We all become equal in the dark earth.

What we think we conquer over this earth
when we sow where we have reaped
are only so many seasons far short of eternity.
We are numbered by the number of our breaths.
We breathe so many, and then there is only death.

And so whatever trophies you have won
and display for all the world to see
will mean no more to you
when in the darkness you find eternity.

For we all come at last to our graves.
Our final rewards.
Breaths of brown dust,
where once we took our breaths above -
above the green, green graveyard grass.

Heaven Is a Communist Country

I don't like Paradise –

Because it's Sunday – all the time –
And Recess – never comes –

~ Emily Dickinson

Heaven is a Communist country run by God. There will be no one there to ask you if you want fries with that burger. If there is, you will know you are in the wrong place. It will be from everyone according to their ability, to everyone according to their need. Since abilities will be limitless, and needs none, this will be an easy standard to meet. Social security will be infinite. Everyone will have paid the required amount into the system. Health care, education, shelter – all will be provided for. Mansions of gold, if you want. All needs will be met, forever. All will be treated fairly, forever. Some may find this disconcerting, and long for the earthly life they left behind, or the hell they successfully avoided. Alas, it will be too late. They will be stuck forever in Heaven, a Communist country run by God.

Last Kiss

The touch of a breath.
The sweet taste of salt.
The perfume of skin.
The silence of a cry.
The sight of the dark.

Last Words

"The reward of great men is that, long after they have died, one is not quite sure that they are dead."

~ Jules Renard
from **The Journal of Jules Renard,** December, 1893
translated from the French by Louise Bogan and Elizabeth Roget

The epitaph.
The voice gone quiet.
Words set in stone.
Our words.
Others' lips.
The dates of our deaths
can be known.
Numbers set in stone.
Names set in stone.
Whatever memories
we have given.
Whatever memories
that we give.
When does the last
memory die?
No one knows.
No recording can be made.
When do we become
the words in the stone?
And then and now –
When do we become
the self no one knows?

Lifewalk

All along
the eternal
tapestry we
walk.
Never knowing
the forever
flight of time,
nor its constant
considered
creation.

Life and Death

Is not the darkness
something?

The light thinks so.

Little Gifts

There are snowflakes, and footprints in the sand,
and your first tooth.
There are sunsets, and the sound of your mother's voice,
and the breath making of your lover,
lying naked beside you.
From the headwater of the womb,
into the ocean of the stars,
there is all the joy we can ever know,
and all the pain we ever need to know.
The best God gives us are metaphors.
The best we can give God is to find them.

Metaphors for Infinity

He could never find the right thing to say.
He could always find the wrong thing to say.
This was not his intention.
His intention was to find some way
to find a way that made some sense.
A way to be specific about life.
In the face of too many specific deaths.
A dog barks on a winter's night.
Ice cubes fall in a glass of whiskey.
That sort of thing.
Infinity manifested.
Infinity in his manifest.
There was none.
Atoms and abstractions.
An abstract God.
That was all.
That was the problem.

My Epitaph

He did not conquer all.

Nights

"Days are where we live."

from *Days*
by Philip Larkin

Nights are where we practice death.
Nights are where we touch our bodies and our hearts where no one can see.
Nights are where we make babies.
Nights are where we worry about days.
Nights are where we dream.
Nights are where we are afraid of the dark.
Nights are all there was before there was a God.
Nights are the goodness into which we should not gently go.
Nights are where we gently pass away.
Nights are where we go after days.
There could be no days without nights.

The Losers' Art

"the art of losing's not too hard to master"

   from *One Art*
   by Elizabeth Bishop

Some of us are lost every day.
The rest of us lose a day every day.

Then we lose a friend, a lover,
a father, a mother,
a husband, a wife,
a son, a daughter,
a sister, a brother.

Till all we become is lost.

If there is a Master of loss,
he has yet to teach us the Master's art.

What do we know?

The words for loss - we know.
The loss for words - we know.

We know the art of words.
We know the loss of words.

Words are what we know.

The Whippoorwills Were Singing

She thought she might sleep
and not wake up.
She had this thought every night.
This night it would be true.

She did not want to die alone.
Neither did she want for others to see her die.

She was ninety-five.
She had not been sick until the last few months.
She was not in pain.

Others would say *it was for the best.*
She lived a long and a good life.
She did not die in pain.
She had a quiet death in the night.
She had the best death anyone could hope for.

She thought there should be
something more.
Some further accounting.

But she was tired,
and tired of thinking.
She closed her eyes.
It was a clear night,
and the whippoorwills were singing.

There Was A Day

There was a day.
Then there was none.
The past everlasting.
Until there is
no one to remember.
All there ever was.
All there ever will be.
I do not think
there can be stories
without endings.
But I would like
for a God
to prove
me wrong.

Whispers in Time

Time is a whisper.
We are time.
We whisper in time.
We are whispers.
We are time in whispers.
We are whispers in time.

www.ingramcontent.com/pod-product-compliance
Lightning Source LLC
Chambersburg PA
CBHW051129160426
43195CB00014B/2399